Journey with
Trust *and* Fire *Within*

Why I Live Life in the Spirit!

Sheila S. Ward

ISBN 978-1-64349-087-8 (paperback)
ISBN 978-1-64349-088-5 (digital)

Christian Faith Publishing, Inc.
832 Park Avenue
Meadville, PA 16335
www.christianfaithpublishing.com

Printed in the United States of America

I dedicate this book to our Blessed Mother Mary
and her son Jesus through the Holy Spirit!

*****

May the breath of God breathe on you,
and make His presence known!

Please note that *** indicates where music was used as part of my witnesses, testimonies, or presentations.

All songs mentioned in this book are part of my albums "Holy Spirit Breath of God" and "Magnificat," which can be listened to or downloaded from my website: www.sheilasward.com.

Contents

Preface

(Walking in faith is not easy, but it is simple.)

*****

Journey with Trust and Fire Within is a small book of why I live life in the Spirit! This small book is a story of my journey, from my upbringing to where I am right now in my life. It includes witnessing chapters of why I live my life in the Spirit, my ritual morning prayers, the vow I have taken, and my personal relationship with the Holy Spirit.

It should be noted while these pages were written in obedience to God, that is not to say every word on each page of these chapters will be the will of God—*absolutely not!* But it is to say these are witnesses of my journey, taken with complete trust in the Lord. Even as I may often fall or take the wrong path, my trust is completely in the Lord, for I know He will lead me to the right path when I make a wrong turn and lift me back up when I fall.

God knows my heart wants to follow His voice where He wills me, and I know He will never leave me to fight my battles alone. Always and forever, God is with me. Always and forever, my trust is in the Lord, my God.

Even if you may not be aware of the Lord working in your life, through the grace and mercy of God, I pray what you read in these pages will help you recognize, experience, and believe in the power of inner prayer and the Holy Spirit in you.

You will hear words of Jesus through scripture and through your own thoughts by having a personal relationship with Him.

You can take all my possessions, but if I hold within me this personal relationship with my Lord—the very breath of God breathing on me, speaking to me in my thoughts—then I have everything. I could not exist without this relationship nor would I want to. Amen!

My Thank-You

First and most importantly, to my precious and most trusted friend the Holy Spirit who is the very reason for this book to exist, to Jesus who gives me my every breath, and to Blessed Mary for helping me say yes.

To my mom and my dad, bless their souls, who were both a great influential part of my early life. Their love continues to reach the center of my heart with inspirations.

To my Irish twin brother, bless his soul, for his never ending love and trust in me.

To Father William J. McCarthy, MSA, who became my spiritual father, and to Sister Bernadette Sheldon, SCJ, who became my spiritual mother, bless her soul. Their powerful words and teachings continue to inspire me to be all I can be and all for the glory of God! I am so blessed to still have this holy priest as my spiritual father in life. Thank you, Lord Jesus!

To my loved ones: my soul mate, John, who is deeply spiritual and has been and continues to be the strength in my weakness, and to my children, Jen and John, who forever will be and always were the joy inside my heart even while so many miles kept us apart.

To all my extended families and friends and all my brothers and sisters in the Lord.

To every person who has ever touched my life in one way or another, I say thank you. Each one of you has a part in helping me be where I am right now. Each person is so very important in fitting together all the pieces to this life we have been so blessed to have. Praise the Lord always and forever!

To my cousin Dolores for her photo of us as youngsters.

To my spiritual sister Huguette for the inside and back cover photos she took at a spiritual concert that was given in honor of Father Bill's birthday at My Father's House Retreat Center.

Lastly, to my spiritual director, Father Bill, for all he does, for who he is, and for his beautiful letter printed on the back cover of this small book.

Opening Prayer

(Jesus, forgive me, a poor sinner,
and have mercy on me.)

*****

Dear Father who art in heaven,
in your holy name and
in the name of your son Jesus,
through the powers of your
Holy Spirit, I ask you please, Lord, bless and touch
each person who is reading the
pages in this book right
now in ways that will speak to each heart and heal
what is needed in them as only you, Lord, know.
I ask you, Lord, enlighten each
person right now to truly

know you in their lives and, with
a willing spirit, to hear
and answer your call in whatever direction
you will for them in their lives.
Thank you, Lord, for hearing my prayer. Amen.

When you surrender to God, to the Lord, to Jesus, you are surrendering to a new life in Jesus, a new life in the Spirit, and with this new life in the Spirit is a personal relationship with God. Yes, with Jesus and you.

I ask each one of you who is reading this right now to slowly pray this prayer and hear each word in your heart as you are praying:

Yes, Lord,
I want a personal relationship with you.
Open my ears, Lord, that I may hear your words.
Open my mouth that I may praise your holy name.
Lord Jesus, help me be all I can
be and all you will me to
be for everyone in my life. In your holy name I pray.
Thank you, Lord, for hearing my prayer.
I love you, Oh Lord, my God! Amen.

Thank you.

While this is my story, there's a story in you. Together with our Blessed Mary, we all can proclaim:

The Lord has done great things for me, Holy is His Name! (Luke1:49)

Feet First ... Here I Come

(My Early Life)

My dad loved telling the story of how he and my mom met. As he would have us believe, my mom tripped him while they were both ice skating in the park one day, and that's how he "fell" in love with my mom.

 They were married in Auburn, Maine, October 1946, at Sacred Heart Catholic Church.

They moved to Bridgeport, Connecticut, where my mom gave birth to their firstborn,

Howard Michael Ward on January 3, 1948. He was baptized at St. Charles Church that same month.

They moved back to Lewiston, Maine, where my mom gave birth to my brother's Irish twin—me.

Feet first, here I come—a breech baby in the cold of December 1948. I was baptized at St. Joseph Church in Lewiston that same month.

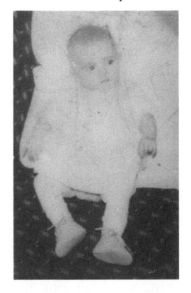

My brother and I were indeed very blessed to have our mom and dad for they were a great influential part of our early life.

We come from a deep-rooted Catholic family. Mom would get us ready for bed, but before we hopped in, Dad would come in and have us kneel on the floor facing the crucifix on the wall over our beds and teach us our prayers. Every night, we would recite the Lord's Prayer, the Hail Mary, the Act of Contrition, and other prayers.

I remember this big old Bible our parents had, which they kept on the bottom shelf of an end table in the parlor. Every now and then, I would see my mom writing in it. They kept all their important papers in the pages specifically marked for this type of information, like baptism, communion, confirmation, holy orders, marriage, divorce, diseases, illnesses, death dates, and so on. Still, I was always confused by what I didn't see. I didn't see any Bible reading, and I didn't hear any either.

In our home, they were not allowed to read the Bible. Now that's silly I know, but that was the way things were before the Second Vatican Council (Vatican II). People were forbidden to read the Bible. They had one, but they were told not to read it.

On Sundays, special days, and whenever we took a car trip, we would recite the Rosary prayers. On Fridays of Lent, our dad would take us to the stations of the cross. So, yes, we were Catholics, and I loved it. All those prayers made me feel safe and loved.

One of my first memories was sitting on my dad's lap at a very young age. Him with his beautiful tenor voice, teaching me to sing the songs he so loved singing, and feeling this strong sense of belonging, which I would soon discover was my passion for music.

Another early memory is from around the age of three. I'm in a dance recital with my brother, cousins, and the other children in my dance class. We're on stage, dancing as we rehearsed all season, but unbeknownst to my dancing teacher, she is about to witness one of her little darlings coming out of formation. As the music was playing, I stopped dancing, walked over to the front in the center of the stage, and started singing with the song that was playing as the rest of my class danced the way we all rehearsed, only this time, without me. It's clear to see singing was definitely taking root in me.

Happy memories as a child were whenever there were family events, my three cousins—little Linda, Dolores, and Margaret—and I would always be at a mic. We loved singing together, but mostly, we just loved being together.

I'm about five in this next memory, which is mixed with sadness and, at the same time, a heavenly Mother's love. I believe without the suffering and sadness, I may not have experienced this heavenly Mother's love.

My brother and I were being kept while our parents were both working in different states, our mom in Maine and our dad in Connecticut. When nighttime came, I was not allowed to sleep upstairs where my brother and the other children were. I had to sleep in the bed on the main floor. I was put into a situation no child could understand, and I would not know until years later why I suffered much pain.

When morning came, I would run out to the backyard of woods and cry to our Blessed Mother Mary with my tiny little silver rosary beads clenched tightly in my hand.

On this particular day, it was windy, and the more I ran, the windier it became. I passed by the chickens and the swing I used to love to swing on. Then I stopped, the wind stopped, and it became dark and still. I looked up, and there I saw ... *a ray of lights coming from a tree. In between its branches was the most beautiful heavenly lady looking at me with the softest sound of silence I have ever heard.* She spoke no words, yet I knew she was my special Blessed Mother.

There are no words that can describe that experience of joy I felt inside my tiny body. It was as though I was being held by the arms of truth, and I knew she would always be there for me. Her memory, to this day, is so alive in me, as though I still have a secret no one can take from me.

From that day on, I was able to hold on to that special moment. Whenever I felt a little sad or unhappy about anything, I would pray to my special Blessed Mother. As I prayed my little prayers, thoughts of the rays of light would appear in my mind, and I would remember my most beautiful heavenly lady looking at me. Then my sadness would disappear, and I would feel her love hold me.

About a year after I saw my most beautiful Blessed Mother, my brother and I attended St. Louis School in Lisbon, Maine, where I seemed to always get myself into trouble.

It was on April Fool's Day when an older classmate told me to fetch the mother superior and tell her she was needed in the second floor classroom for something about April Fool's. I didn't really understand since I was only in kindergarten, but I did as the older girl asked.

When the mother superior and I got to the classroom, it was empty. She asked me why the classroom was empty, and I told her I didn't know and they said it was April Fool's. She wasn't happy with me and took me into the office and literally tied me to a chair with ribbons. Now that didn't hurt, but to make things worse, she asked me for my parent's name and I said Mommy and Daddy. Then she asked what names they called each other, and I said *honey* and *darling*. This lasted through the recess, so I didn't get to play that day. She sent a note home with my brother to give to my parents, and my mom went to see her the very next day. You can say this was just one of those typical upbringing issues, I guess.

My brother made his first Holy Communion and his confirmation simultaneously in May 1955 at St. Louis Church while he was seven.

In April 1956, when I was seven, I also made my first Holy Communion, but I was older when I made my confirmation.

I was still seven when we moved from Maine to Talcott Street, New Britain, Connecticut, in an apartment building facing the school we would be attending. However, our move did not keep us from going back to Maine often for visits.

We had a big family with many family get-togethers. It seemed visiting and keeping in touch with our families (cousins Sandy, Diane, Jackie, Pauline, Mike, and Jeanie, just to name a few of the Bussieres on my mom's side, not to mention my three singing cousins, and cousins Kim, Peggy, Connie, Marcel, and my dear Janice, just to name a few of the Wards on my dad's side) were a big part of our lives, with these being the cousins we hang around with mostly.

There are so many cousins that I would not be able to name them all, but oh, how I remember always looking forward to our next events. Our visits would include cousins, aunts, uncles, grandparents (my mom's parents), and Reverend Bourque and my grandmother (my dad's stepmom) who was the cook and housekeeper for Reverend Bourque in the rectory where she lived in Lisbon. Reverend Bourque would take my brother and me to the church and give us prayer cards and tell us stories all about the saints. He was so interesting.

Once we were moved into our apartment, my parents tried to get us into St. Mary's Catholic School, but they were not able to take us because my brother and I only spoke French. However, St. Mary's Church still became our parish, and three years later, in October 1959, I made my confirmation there. I was ten years old.

1960

When I was eleven, we moved from the apartment building into our own home where I befriended my lifelong soul sister, Missy, who is very dear to me. I also befriended a girl named Kathy. Missy and I would call her Red because she had such beautiful red hair.

At fourteen, I attended St. Maurice Junior High where the nuns were stern, but I had a great love for them and thought of becoming a singing nun. Actually, the mother superior gave me that idea. I was also part of the children's choir at St. Maurice's Church.

Later, I joined two teenage rock 'n' roll bands, The Night Riders (the leader of this band was Missy's brother Tony) and the other band was called The Shades with Little Sheila. I loved being in both these bands.

Once, while visiting in Maine, I had an opportunity to be a guest singer in my cousin Connie's cousin Ron's band at a dance held in Augusta, Maine.

I just loved being a teenager, meeting and singing with so many different bands.

It seemed my teen years were also preparing me for my music ministry ahead, but I thought I was just doing what everyone did—write songs and sing.

I used to do this often on long walks or bike rides or when I'm just off into the woods alone; I would sing to my Blessed Mother and Jesus.

1965-1968

I befriended a special classmate from the school I loved most. My friend's name is Julie, and the school was Mary Immaculate Academy (MIA) of New Britain, Connecticut. It was an all-girls Catholic high school.

Somewhere near the end of that first year at MIA, I was so excited about an event that took place, and I couldn't wait to tell Julie about it. I caught up with her in the hallway and said, "Julie, yesterday, my dad took Missy and me to the bowling alley, and I met this cute boy named Neil." Then the bell rang, and off to class we went.

Now when it was lunchtime and we were in the cafeteria, Julie said to me, "So do you like him?"

I looked at her and said, "Julie, I'm going to marry him."

She looked back at me and asked, "Now how would you know that?"

I said, "I don't know, but I will."

Then off we went into the chapel, as we did most days at school, and prayed our Rosary together before our afternoon classes.

I remember many times Julie coming with me to my teenage rock 'n' roll band practices and how I loved that so much. We went everywhere together. It was especially fun just hanging out and wondering what our future held for us.

We looked forward to Graduation, we just didn't realize that we would be graduating from different schools, Julie received her diploma from MIA but my 12th grade was split, attending the first half at, NBHS, New Britain High School of New Britain, Connecticut, then finishing my studies at home through the US Mail and receiving my diploma from American High School of Chicago, Illinois.

I left the school I loved best because I learned that Sister Mary, C.F.M., who had been tutoring and helping me in my studies had left MIA and became a. teacher at NBHS. She was a Mentor to me and I thought I could have her for my teacher again if I went to NBHS, but I never saw her there, I never saw her again.

Instead I was in a large school, so different from MIA, without any friends. It was wall to wall kids. The classes were overly filled with boys and girls. I basically felt alone and cast out. I was becoming more and more withdrawn. My parents thought it best to pull me out of NBHS and I finished my studies at home through the mail.

I wished I never left MIA, for sure I made a bad decision. Julie and I drifted into different directions following our own path into a new beginning.

New Beginning

April 1969

Neil and I were married at the Army base in Fort Dix, New Jersey. A short time later, he was sent to Vietnam.

When I was twenty-one, I gave birth to my first baby in February 1970. Such a precious beautiful blessing!

When Jennifer was only three months old, I received a vision while on a jet plane coming back home from my husband's R&R trip in Hawaii. It was not a happy one, and I shared it with my soul sister, Missy. Although she tried comforting me, two weeks later, it happened, just as I shared it with Missy.

The troops were in an army helicopter, hovering close to the ground while the men were jumping out, and as my husband jumped out, he was shot to the ground by an armor-piercing bullet, ripping open his chest.

I received a phone call about him from his mom. He was not killed—praise God—but he was, however, severely injured and was sent to the VA hospital in New York.

I dropped the phone and ran to my bedroom where my baby was sleeping. Then I grabbed and held her tightly in my arms and gazed upon the statue of my Blessed Mother Mary. At that very moment, my bedroom filled me with thoughts of the rays of light coming back to me from when I was much younger and the feeling I received as I embraced that same feeling of the sweet soft silence I experienced before.

My brother, being worried, opened my door. I handed him my baby, Jennifer, and went off to church to pray and to thank my Blessed Mother Mary for being not only with me but also with my baby's father.

I knew Neil was going to be fine. He was getting good care, not to mention all the overflowing prayers he was receiving.

In September 1971, I gave birth to our second child. Another beautiful precious blessing!

Here, Jennifer is eighteen months and lovingly holding her infant baby brother, Johnny.

The Lord has greatly blessed us, and forever I will praise His holy name for our daughter and son.

Early to Midseventies

I was breaking down. I was feeling alone again, and some of my childhood memories were now haunting me.

Remember in the previous chapter where my brother and I were being kept while our parents were both working in different states?

Now I wanted to know why I had to sleep down-stairs and why I would hurt so much.

I do come from a "typical" Catholic family, where things of sadness are not spoken, so I really had no one believing me nor in me, including and especially my immediate family. But I needed to know, and this is the story they told to me:

> You see, Sheila, when you were about five years old, you fell from the kitchen counter onto the pointed part of a rocking chair.
>
> We had to take you to the hospital where they stitched you up, but you needed a lot of medicine.
>
> When you and Howie were being kept you had to sleep on the main floor because whoever was keeping you needed to rub a pasty medicine on the lower tailbone part of your body, and that was very painful for you.

Well, I had a very difficult time understanding their explanation. I felt my inside crying out for help, but none would come. I became, instead, withdrawn, and the psychiatric doctor in whose care I was placed (I will call him Dirks) apparently enjoyed finding new medication to try on his patients. Unfortunately, I became one of Dirks's guinea pigs for some of his experiments.

Dirks told me I would be there in the hospital for a very long time. He also made me believe my own brother raped me. He had me on a medicine that gave me terrible worthless thoughts of myself where life for me was becoming not lived, and instead, I was existing solely for Dirks's experimental drugs.

I tried leaving many times but was always found and brought back to the hospital. One of those times was when I left the hospital and walked to the main street area of Middletown. I used the pay phone from a corner tavern to call my husband to come take me home. He tried talking to me, but the communication was cut off. Then I called a friend and waited for my ride.

While waiting, I noticed a police cruiser pulling up to park in the front. Three large police officers came out, and I just knew it had to be for me. I looked for the back door, but none was to be found. Then I went to the ladies' room and waited there in hopes they would leave.

They didn't. Instead, a loud shout came from the other side of the door telling me I needed to come out and go with them. I felt like a criminal as I was being taken away, one holding each arm and the third walking directly behind me. We walked past my riders as they watched the officers put me into the back of the cruiser. Really now, three large officers? I was four feet and ten and half inches at ninety-five pounds.

Then back to the hospital. There didn't seem to be any escaping from Dirks's drugs or what it was doing to me. There were more hospital stays and a few times of trying to end my life. Never knowing what thoughts were real, where I'm going, or even where I was at any given time, not to mention the horrible nightmares of my life ending in tragic ways.

Dirks kept me in his control, making me feel unworthy of anything that was good. My children are good, so I must be unworthy of being their mom. My husband was good, again, I must be unworthy to be his wife and so on were the thoughts that kept coming.

To this day, I may never know to what extent Dr. Dirks suppressed my memory or the damage that lay hidden in his drugs, but after the many attempts of trying to leave, I had no hope of life beyond that dark depression I was in.

The doctor not only upped my medications to keep me from leaving again but also tried one of his new pills. By morning, I was unresponsive. The nurse couldn't even find a pulse, and though it seemed I was unconscious and dying, I could hear everything going on although I was not able to tell them. My body was totally unresponsive. I even heard the nurse say, "I think she's dead."

The inside of me kept screaming out to them, "I'm not dead! I'm not dead!"

Scary? It was absolutely terrifying!

It did, however, create a lot of attention. They wheeled me in a room full of nurses and doctors. This lasted through the night into days, and finally, after three days, they were able to bring my body back to respond. However, due to my very low white blood cell count, they had to take a bone marrow sample to try to fix whatever went wrong. I guess that's what happens when you're a guinea pig.

That road was leading me into the darkness of no return.

One day, my mom—bless her soul—saved me from the hands of those who had me in bondage. Off to the psych ward this little lady went, searching until she found me and took me home. She then made it clear to everyone I was not to return there. She was so strong. Her love was so deep!

I'm not sure how she did all that, but I do believe she knew through her prayers what she needed to do and somehow received strength from our Blessed Mother Mary to save me. Through the grace and mercy of God, save me she did. My mom saved me, and she helped me through that part of my life.

It took a while but then I started to feel better. No more pills, no more experiments, and most importantly, no more Dirks or being Dirks's guinea pig.

My mom wanted me to see a specialist. I did, and this specialist doctor said the medicines Dr. Dirks had me on were for people with hallucinations. In my case, not being in that category, it would eventually make me "insane" and create even more complications.

Now all this might have been prevented if I had sought a second doctor's opinion. Obviously, Dr. Dirks was not the right choice of psychiatrist and, in truth of the matter, was a bad doctor due to his evaluations being based on his different kinds of medicine research and not a true evaluation to see how he can help me instead of using me in his research. So a second and even a third doctor's opinion is so important.

Please, if you have a situation in your life, don't discount all doctors because of one bad doctor. Most doctors—psychiatry or any other branch of medicine—are there to help you. There are good and bad in all line of professions, and it's not always easy.

Keep in mind doctors are like vehicles, where some are too small while others are very large. You cannot get five people from one place to another in a two-passenger car, just as you cannot have medicine for a headache curing heart problems. Neither will work. Three people from that small car will be left behind, and the heart problem will go untreated.

God wants the very best for you and the best in your life. Ask God to help in all directions and especially when seeking the right doctor for you in your own situation. When something doesn't feel right, it usually means it isn't right. Don't give up, and don't lose hope. Keep asking God to lead you. You will know when He does. Then believe and trust in the promptings of God inside you.

At that time in my life, I didn't know God was there for me or that I could ask Him to help me. I wish I knew, but I didn't. I want you to know you can! Jesus loves you. He already died for you so you could have life to the fullest. God always is there for you. He waits for you.

Because I still walked with blinders on my eyes and deaf ears, the Lord helped me through my mom. Moms, as I've been told, always pray for their children. I am so thankful to the Lord for using my mom to save me. Bless my mom's soul. I do miss her so much.

As far as what really happened when my brother and I were being kept, I will probably never know the truth, only the memories of a child's pain, for as I mentioned before, I may never know to what extent Dr. Dirks suppressed my memory nor the damage that lay hidden in his drugs.

Unfortunately, it took more than a decade of healing before I discovered the truth about my brother although, deep in my heart, I wanted this to be another of Dr. Dirks's lies. And it was! That bad doctor had ways of twisting the brain in many different directions. Let me tell you, Dirks caused my family a lot of hardship and suffering, but I know this: *my brother Howard was a brother to be loved, not feared. He was the best brother any sister could ever have, and I thank God for him and miss him so much. Bless his soul.*

If you are as blessed as I was to have someone who sees something is wrong and wants to either get you out of someone's care or have a second and even a third doctor's opinion, then please accept their help and follow their lead for they are a true blessing in your life, just like my mom was in my life.

As my healing started, I received prayer support from all the right places and started to follow my own heart of prayers.

Baby Christian
(Baby Steps into Healing)

Mid to Late Seventies

Between my mom's rescue and receiving prayer support from all the right places, this baby Christian was on the pathway of baby steps into healing.

I met my first special sister in the Lord in 1978. Her name is Gwen. She was the music director in our church, and I was a part of her choir. She is one of the best music directors I have ever been blessed to know. Gwen also became my first prayer partner, teaching me to pray the Breviary and Office of Readings and taking me to prayer groups. Oh, how I loved those prayer groups; so uplifting and so much a need in my healing.

Healing brings awareness which is what it did for me on our family vacation at the Cape. I was feeling so aware of God's presence.

It was Wednesday, August 22, 1979. We were sitting on the beach of Marconi.

Jen and John were busy building their sandcastles. The waves weren't as high as they were in the morning, but the glorious certainties of the unknown were still in the clutches of their never ending grip.

God's love of nature seemed to be all around—a low airplane over the tops of the waves, children tasting the salt with their lips in the air, Frisbees and footballs being passed back and forth, homemade kites in the overhead winds, and three heads on the sand—or I should say *in* the sand, for their bodies were covered to their necks with the white sand of the beach. Such a wonder in the sights of love all around. There are so many thanks to be given to God our Almighty Father and Creator that it's hard to know where to begin. There is no end to the thanks that should be given.

When I became aware of all the thanks that should be given Him, the joy of God's peace overflowed within me so generously, and the beauty of God's love surrounded me endlessly. The blinders were removed from my eyes, and the clarity of under-standing brought such delight within my being.

Just like the delightful happening we received that evening when we took Jen and John to the drive-in movies to see *The Muppet Show*. We put the backseat of our station wagon down so they could see without any problems and be comfortable with their pillows and blankets. While watching *The Muppets* Johnny asked me to move over to the right, and of course, thinking I must be blocking his view, I moved. I asked him if it was okay after moving over to where he wanted me to be. He said yes, but his voice sounded like he was directly behind me so, curiously, I turned around to see why he wanted me to move in front of his view. Well, I wasn't blocking his view but the view of all his stuffed animal friends, which he had lined up so they could see *The Muppet Show*. I was blocking their view.

Such beauty for us to see. God's love truly is everywhere. I thanked the Lord for those precious moments. The Lord is in all His children's inner dreams. His presence among them comes forth in rays of His love beaming as bright as burning flames. I will thank my Lord forever and always!

It seemed like awareness became stronger in me during that beautiful vacation. On our way home, as I was writing and thanking the Lord in my journal, I found my heart receiving this poem. A poem for my Lord (August 25, 1979, Saturday, on our way home from the Cape):

Thank You, My Dear Lord

Thank you, my dear Lord, for all we've seen and done
for what we've learned, for chill-some winds
for warm rays from the sun.

For sufferings I feel within my heart
for songs that tear my thoughts apart
for uncertain feelings of where I belong
for not knowing my life when the radio's on.

Oh Lord, how my heart would cry so inside
to feel your presence near
to give me strength I needed so
to dry away my tears.

Then I'd see Johnny's funny little smile
and there your signs would be
in his words, in his acts, and even in his tease.

Jen would always be on guard
she seemed to catch my mood
she'd grab my hand, I'd feel her touch
I knew it came from you.

All the battles I've encountered
between the good and bad
I knew when satan was at work
by twisted thoughts I had.

But then, my Lord, you'd speak to me
through man, one of your sons
with love, my man would hold my hand
I knew that good had won.

I left this camp trip in your hands
to guide us with your plans
space 418 you had reserved
from end, it was the third.

So, Lord, with all my heart, I say
thank you for this day
thank you, Lord, for this week
for making it complete.

Lord, thank you for all year
for always being here
for summer, fall, winter, spring
my Lord, for everything
for all the people that I know
for those I have not met
for Christian brothers and sisters too
and memories I can't forget.

I thank you, my dear Lord,
for all I have and all I am
and, Lord, I say to you
all I have and all I am,
I offer all to you.

Your instrument, I want to be
your signs, please show to me
my life is yours, do as you will
do with me, Lord, as you will.

With all my heart, my soul, and mind
I love you, my dear Lord, you gave me life
you gave me love, you opened for me doors
and so, again, I say to you, thank
you, my dear Lord. Amen.

It seemed like I could not contain my feelings within me. When we returned home from our vacation, I felt a hunger and longing for the Lord that kept growing deeper. I continued going to prayer groups with Gwen. She would pray with me even on the phone whenever I needed. She's such a special blessing in my life.

I was writing more praise music and songs, and knowing my love for music, Gwen told me of a priest who also shared this love for music and held prayer meetings every Wednesday morning. It was called the "Holy Spirit Breakfast," given by Fr. William J. McCarthy, MSA, and Sister Bernadette Sheldon, SCJ.

One Wednesday morning, I found myself going to my first Holy Spirit Breakfast. Father Bill and Sister Bernadette started the meeting with John 15:9: "As the Father has loved Me, I have also loved you. Remain in My love."

I felt my heart burning for the Lord. I knew healing touched me, and I was on fire! I knew from that very moment, it was the beginning of living my life in the *Spirit*! For me, there is no turning back!

Why I Live Life in the Spirit
(No Turning Back)

This chapter begins with our Blessed Mary's song of praise: the Magnificat (Luke 1:46–55). In this prayer, I have included my aspiration hymn prayer before and after Mary's canticle because here I am asking for Blessed Mary to also help me proclaim with her in her Magnificat. That in doing so, I also can proclaim God's goodness in my own life.

Aspiration hymn prayer: "Blessed Mary, help me to proclaim with you in your Magnificat!"

"The Magnificat"—Luke 1:46–55

***

In September 1979, as I mentioned previously, I went to my first Holy Spirit Breakfast and met Fr. Bill McCarthy, MSA, and a very special nun, Sr. Bernadette Sheldon, SCJ, bless her soul.

Sister Bern and I formed a bond instantly, and she would call me her special friend. Both Sister Bern and Father Bill would later become my spiritual father and mother. I was drawn to their prayer meetings and teachings from the first moment I walked in. They were teaching on the power of inner prayer, the many ways to hear God speaking to us, daily readings from the Bible, the importance of keeping a spiritual journal, God speaking in our thoughts, and having a personal relationship with Jesus! This touched me deeply; simple yet powerful teachings I could not live without. The more I received, the more I needed to receive.

These two holy people opened the door of my understanding into the Holy Spirit empowering my life! I discovered the Holy Spirit wasn't just "in the name of the Father and of the Son and of the Holy Spirit. Amen." *No!* Not even close!

The Holy Spirit became alive in me. The very breath of God breathed into me. The Holy Spirit became my most precious and closest friend, teacher, comforter, and my life! I started keeping my own spiritual journal, reading scriptures, and speaking to my Savior in prayer. I sang songs of longing and thirsting for Jesus to breathe His holy will into me. I kept wanting more and more. For me, there was absolutely no turning back. Every morning, I found myself in my little prayer area, sometimes in the early morning hours before anyone was up.

With my Bible, journal, and pen at hand, I would start with prayers like the Our Father or the Act of Contrition, then reading scriptures, praising His holy name within my heart, and finally, quietly listening for His soft voice within my thoughts. I was becoming more aware of God's presence, God's grace and mercy, God's words, and God's unconditional love.

Yet I was like a baby, just learning all about this listening to God stuff. I found myself doing as Sister Bern would teach me, asking the Holy Spirit every-thing, putting the Holy Spirit in my everyday life, and seeking the will of God. It was as though I had a secret—a very special gift—and I needed to take this gift and use it, try it out, and believe—really believe—it. Sister Bern said, "Ask of the Holy Spirit anything, and believe in the answers you receive." So I did.

As I practiced this form of prayer, I received more insight. I was learning to live in the Spirit, to trust in the Spirit, to listen to the Spirit, and to joyfully have this relationship with Jesus that even through suffer-ing, I could rejoice as I find myself seeking the Lord in all things.

In my morning prayer, I would hear the Lord ask of me to either *go there, do this, call this person,* and more—endlessly more. I would do as instructed for I knew it was our Lord Jesus Christ, through His Holy Spirit, that was leading me. How did I know? Because I was becoming more aware of the Holy Spirit's prompt-ings. How did I know the voice of God? Because it was within me. It wasn't a voice I heard with my ears. What I heard was God's ever-so-soft voice in my very own thoughts where my whole being would feel this is God! God's voice was in my thoughts.

Holy Scripture tells us in John 10:27: "My sheep hear My voice, I know them, and they follow Me."

One day, I was praying in St Gregory's Church as I was going through difficult times. I asked the Lord to send someone to me. I was also feeling a need to put the deepest part of me on the cross with Jesus, so I took my little silver rosary beads I received from my aunt and uncle's wedding when I was their flower girl. I've had it since I was age five, and I put it on the cross with Jesus. It would remain there for five years.

I continued to pray. Then my dear friend Gwen who was not coming to the church found herself turning her car around from where she was going and headed for that church even while she had no reason or any idea why. But she too recognized the promptings of the Holy Spirit.

Another time in prayer, I was asked to go to Bridgeport to pick up an office prayer book about an hour away, so I took my map and off I went.

On my return, still using the map, I prayed for the Lord to let me get back in time for my children getting off the school bus. I barely had an hour left. Then I heard, "Let go of the map, and let me be in control."

I did. I listened, and I returned in time for my children. Praise the Lord!

I am always in awe of the Lord but never in disbelief. More like, yes, Lord! I know this is you! I know your voice, and I will follow!

Yes, there are many times when I will question my thoughts, but clarity comes as wisdom reaches deep into your being, making you more aware of the Holy Spirit's promptings. That is why it is so important to have a personal relationship with our Lord. Through our daily thirst for Him, we become more and more aware of the promptings of the Holy Spirit!

I found my prayer life taking a deeper root. I was writing even more songs for the Lord, singing more praises, from retreats to churches to wherever God would send me.

I didn't know it at the time, but what I was having was a personal relationship with my heavenly Father, my merciful Jesus, my precious Holy Spirit, my God! A personal relationship with my Lord, wow! Now that takes my breath away!

This gift is real! Everywhere I go, I know I have the Holy Spirit, my personal friend, empowering me, guiding my life into truth, and helping me live my life in the Spirit.

1980 – to 1984

On a camping trip one weekend, in July 1980, my children's father was a little upset when he could not start the kerosene burner. I said to him, "Ask God to help you, and He will," but he continued to try his way.

Then he pushed it toward me and said, "You ask God."

His anger did not subside because I did ask God, and yes, you know it, God helped me light the kerosene burner.

During this same camping trip, we stopped at a walking trail park, and as we were walking, my son ran ahead of us. Then the dream I had the night before came to my mind, so I called out for Johnny to stop and wait for us. In my dream, Johnny was walking across a bridge over water and rocks, and one of the side boards was loose enough where a child Johnny's age could easily fall through. But that was my dream. Still, as we approached the bridge, we found it exactly that way. We stayed till help arrived, and no one was hurt. Praise God! God is so good!

On our way home from this camping trip, as I was sitting back silently praying, I found myself writing this poem to Jesus:

The Mysteries of Your Mountains, Lord

The beauty of your mountains, Lord
the details of their boundaries

they outline all the wonders
of their unknown mysteries
For in the center of their depths
are mighty truths untold
as in the blessed Trinity
to us remains unknown

In the depths of every notch
is a whisper of your love
the peaks of every mountain
shouts your joys from up above
A mystery we cannot see
and yet we know it's there
for in our hearts we do believe
You're with us everywhere

And even when the misty clouds
fills the mountaintops
I still can see all your love
coming down on us
The distance that my eyes can see
on a sunny day
could not begin to justify
the glory of its rays

But knowing that no matter what my eyes
shall rest upon
I see your love embracing us
and keeping us a bond
The stillness of a summer breeze
cooling off the night
will add suspense as we await
upon your mountain high

To gaze into the setting sun
beaming flames so bright
our hearts will forever keep
these memories alive
And so I praise you
Lord of might
for all your wondrous sights!
Amen.

But it wasn't only sunshine and rainbows. I believe in recognizing God's goodness and beauty, you also become more aware of God's sadness. I know the sadness I sometimes would feel deep inside me was not mine. Some were too deep for anything I could experience on my own. Like the Christmas season of 1980.

I was reflecting on the crucified Christ, and because I was no stranger to writing letters to the newspaper (I've written once before, and this would not be the last), again the Bristol Press received from me yet another little corner story for their newspaper.

Here's the actual clipping from the paper:

Christmas Reflection

If it were we, that was with Christ, would He have been crucified? Well, because it was foretold, in scriptures of long ago, we must say yes. And because of this, we feel no guilt. But would we crucify? Would we right now, you and I, inflict pain,, (physically or mentally), as in the time of Christ? Can we honestly examine our conscience and feel right about our actions?

They crucified Christ, and yet saw no wrong in Him. He spoke only truth, He gave His love to all, He was . . . He is . . . and He forever will remain . . . love, and so . . . love . . . was crucified! But not destroyed! For love keeps coming you know, in many different forms. Do we still not know what to do with love? Are we to do as they did? Turn away when love speaks to us? It hurts us so to know that love was crucified; and yet, the hurt keeps getting deeper; for in the mist of our confusions, we pay no mind to our misdoings!

In one status we see someone new to fill a position of a job. This job might be . . . Teaching, Typing, Music Director, Mechanic, a new Priest, Electrician, a Messenger, a Director of Religious Education, or whatever, it doesn't matter what the position is. But do we, in any way at all, take notice, that this person is trying her best and doing a good job? Do we notice that she speaks only truth and has much to offer? This person is . . . love! But what do we do with . . . . love?

As Christians we would open our hearts up wide, and show that we care, and offer our help if needed. We would not look for faults, or compare this new person with the one we grew attached to, for as Christians we would know that Christ works differently in everyone. Look at His twelve Apostles, no two were the same. So let your hearts not harden, but let's instead, rejoice!

Sheila W. Skinnon
Bristol.

I know it was around the same time I wanted so much to know not only His will in my life but also His joy and His sadness. I know God answered my prayer for I was experiencing both sadness and joy far greater and deeper that my tears at times were confusingly uncontrollable, so I knew it was not of me nor from me but of and from Him who willed my prayer to me.

One day, in the late morning hours, I received this message in prayer: "Go to St. Ann's Church in New Britain. There you will find a small boy crying and all alone in church. Go to him, comfort him, and wait with him until his mother returns to take him home." I did. I got in my car, went to St. Ann's, and found the small boy alone and crying. I went over to comfort him. He looked at me through his tears and asked, 'will you stay here with me?' I sat down beside him and told him he was the reason I was there, to stay with him until his mom came for him. I do not know how or why he was there, only that he would be. When his mom got there she seemed so relieved to see her son who was missing for hours, from where or how I do not know. She held her son close to her as she thank me, I told her it was God and then I heard her say, thank you Lord.

On the way home, as I was singing His praises, I had this overwhelming feeling that soon I would be singing and ministering for Jesus in places I have not yet been. Singing is part of who I was since I was just a child, but singing for Jesus and doing God's will gave me such joy I cannot describe.

Oh, how I longed to do this, but the Lord gives to us a little at a time—no more, no less. Even when we want more, it has to come in God's timing.

Sister Bernadette asked me at the following Holy Spirit Breakfast to give a witness and sing the songs the Lord gave me. I did as she asked.

Sister Bern asked me to sing on her biweekly radio show. I did as she asked.

Sister Bern asked me to ask the Holy Spirit to teach me to play my guitar, and yes, I did as she asked.

One day, in the middle of my living room floor, all alone with my guitar, I asked the Holy Spirit to teach me how to play. I tried on my own so many times before, but it seemed so hard to strum with one hand, play the chords with the other hand, and top that off with singing. To me, it was seemingly impossible. Still, I knew all things are possible with Jesus, so I sat on the floor quietly, slowly breathing in and out the name Jesus.

Then I heard His soft voice say, "Play 'Amazing Grace,' my small one. Sing to me and play."

I did as Jesus asked. The room was suddenly still, and I felt as though I was covered with the arms of the Father, the Son, and the Holy Spirit as if being baptized in the Holy Spirit. I didn't see the living room as any kind of room at all. I didn't see anything but what seemed to have been a heavenly covering of love itself.

When I came back from that heavenly covering of love to the living room, I knew what I experienced was not something that could easily be explained. I journalized it and shared it with Sister Bernadette. She shared it with Father Bill, and they prayed about it and later shared with me that it was part of a "mystic life in Jesus."

I was in love with love itself. God is love, and God was breathing on me new life in the Spirit.

I continued my morning ritual and going to Father Bill and Sister Bern's teachings every Wednesday. On one Wednesday, Sister Bernadette and Father Bill were teaching on the importance of staying focused on the Lord; to be strong as to not allow the evil one to rob us of God's gifts. The closer in prayer you are to Jesus, the more the devil will try to stop and rob you, but I was convinced nothing was going to get in my way of following the Lord.

One day, we (my little family and I) thought we would surprise my dad. He had a lot of wood to split for his fireplace. So off we went to my parent's home. I was inside the house, and Jennifer and Johnny were outside with their dad who was splitting a cord of firewood for my dad. Johnny came running in, screaming, "Dad needs you, Mom! Dad needs you!"

I went outside and wrapped a towel around Neil's bloody arms, and we rushed him to the emergency room at the hospital. The doctor took Neil into surgery, and my children and I waited in the waiting room. As I was praying for him and his doctor, I had a sense he would be fine. However, within minutes of that, I also felt something was wrong with my dad. I couldn't shake that feeling. I prayed for him and my mom. I tried calling from the hospital, but no one answered. Still, I had a strong feeling my dad was in trouble. I prayed more.

Later that night, talking on the phone with my mom, I found out what had happened. My dad was assaulted and robbed at gunpoint. He was thrown into the backseat of his own car, about to be kidnapped. As the car was moving, my dad opened the door and fell out, the thieves did not stop. A very kind lady saw him on the ground and helped him into her car, then took him to the hospital. God bless you, Mrs. Stewart, for caring for my dad. When I got off the phone with my mom, I knelt down in prayer to thank God for sparing the lives of my dad and my children's dad. I stood up with conviction and said, "I rebuke you, satan, in the name of the Father and of the Son and of the Holy Spirit and cast you, satan, into the netherworld never to return. Amen!"

Then, back on my knees, I prayed a prayer to the Father, Son, and the Holy Spirit, and this new hymn was created at that very moment.

"Praise You, Blessed Trinity"

***

Praise you, Father. Praise you, Jesus. Praise you, Holy Spirit. Praise you, blessed Trinity!

After a while, when I would think of what happened to my dad, I would get trapped at a place in my life where unpleasant thoughts were crowding my mind, leaving me feeling lost and alone. I didn't like this feeling inside me.

Was I supposed to forgive those who hurt me? Was I supposed to forgive those who hurt my family? Forgiveness was settling in my thoughts, but I didn't know what to do with it. Let me rephrase that: I did know what to do with it. I just wasn't sure I could.

One morning, after sending my children off to school, going to morning Mass, and returning home, I placed myself, as I had many times before, in my little "prayer area" off the kitchen where I could pray, listen, and journalize my conversations with the Lord. As you know, this was a ritual for me. Understanding the ways of hearing God's voice was becoming clearer to me, and as I pondered on the word I was receiving in my thoughts—*forgiveness*—I asked the Lord, "Help me, Father, in my unbelief." I knew there was so much more I needed to learn and understand.

Later that day, in the early evening hours, I had a prayer meeting to go to at a little church building. Prayers were offered, and we were able to go up to the front and ask for anything we want to be prayed for. I did just that. I asked for the gift of "discernment of spirits." People prayed over me. I felt my body gently fall back and lower to the floor. This was my first experience of being "baptized in the Spirit" or "releasing of the Spirit." I remembered thinking, "Are you here, Lord?" Then I saw with the eyes of my heart again.

This was the Lord's invisible covering of love as I heard Him say to me, "I love you, my child. Be not afraid. I will always stand by you, and you will have discernment of spirits. You are mine."

With joyful, tear-filled eyes, I stood up, went back to my seat, and praised God my Savior!

Forgiveness was also becoming clear to me now, and I knew in my heart what I needed to do. So I prayed, "Lord help me forgive Dr. Dirks. Help me forgive the bad men who took my dad and hurt him. Help me forgive everyone who has ever hurt me or my family in anyway. And, Lord, please help me forgive myself from any hurt I may have caused to anyone."

I needed to be forgiving as well as forgiven. To be forgiving, I also needed to seek forgiveness, and now I realized seeking forgiveness had to come from the depths of my being. Things were changing on the inside of me, and I knew what I needed to do.

When I got home that evening, I went over to my little nine-year-old son and said, "Johnny, I am so sorry I yelled at you before leaving. Please forgive me."

He looked at me with an expression of confusion in his delightful eyes as he softly answered yes. I then hugged him and thanked him and told him I love him. Then I went over to my ten-year-old daughter and said to her, "Jennifer, please forgive me for getting angry with you. You didn't do anything wrong, and I am so sorry."

With her beautiful turquoise eyes, she looked back at me and said, "Sure, Mom."

I hugged her and said thank you as I told her how much I love her.

Now I needed to seek forgiveness from my husband, slightly more difficult, although to this day, I am still not clear of what his understanding of it really was when he said, "Fine." He did, however, agree with my thoughts on our children. I needed to use a much softer way of getting through to them. Soft-spoken and more understanding are exactly how I needed to be, and from that day, I became someone I liked. I not only learned to seek forgiveness and forgive; this softer approach also gave my children the gift of listening and me a gift of understanding and forgiveness. We need to be quiet to be able to hear the Lord's voice within our inner thoughts so we don't miss what God wants to tell us. This also became true with me and my children. They needed quietness to hear what I was saying, and I needed to be softer for them to hear me.

The Lord was showing me the power of forgiveness. The Lord's Prayer was becoming alive in me. I understood the true meaning of this beautiful prayer. The Lord opened my mind and gave me wisdom deep into this prayer. This prayer truly has power. Forgiveness is very powerful. Forgiveness is a powerful gift!

It seemed the more I received, the more I wanted to receive. I wanted to know more and more and more.

As I took the Lord's Prayer and listened to each word wholeheartedly, I began to understand this powerful gift we have been given from Jesus.

Forgiveness

In the holy Gospel of Matthew 6:9–13, the Lord's Prayer, *Jesus* gives us a powerful tool in His beautiful

WHY I LIVE LIFE IN THE SPIRIT

prayer. It's not just from start to finish an "Our Father who art in heaven, forgive me …" sorrowful type of prayer, but rather it starts with:

1st: Praising the Lord (*"Our Father who art in heaven, Hallowed be Your name"*)

2nd: The giving of ourselves, all we have and all we are, to God (*"Your kingdom come, Your will be done on earth as it is in heaven"*)

3rd: We are asking God to give us what we need for our journey (*"Give us this day our daily bread"*)

4th: This one is hard, but it cleanses and heals us (*"Forgive us our trespasses, as we forgive those who trespass against us"*). If we are true to ourselves, we know this is difficult but so needed for our own lives to experience healing and cleansing that comes from it in our lives and those around us. In Matthew chapter 6, Jesus tells us, "If you will forgive others their sins, your heavenly Father also will forgive you your sins. But if you will not forgive others, neither will your Father forgive you your sins" (verses 14,15).

Forgiveness is a gift. It cleanses; it heals. I remember a teaching on forgiveness where the instructor had us turn to the person near to us and say, "I'm sorry. Forgive me." When it came to my turn, I began to understand this exercise.

5th: (*"And lead us not into temptation"*) This is our personal prayer to God so we may be able to endure our trials. Jesus Himself prayed to His Father for strength when He was led into the desert to be tempted by the devil. We need to remember the Lord is always with us, and He will never leave us to fight our perils alone.

6th: (*"But deliver us from evil"*) Here we are asking God to cast the enemy from our lives. We pray for God's protection in our lives and in the lives of those around us. Through the grace and mercy of God, we are able to pray and command: "I command you, evil spirit, to be gone from my life, never to return, and I pray this in the name of the Father and of the Son and of the Holy Spirit. Amen." Believe in your heart every word you pray with conviction. Halleluiah!

7th: Joy, peace, and cries of the heart that come from praising the Lord (*"For Yours is the kingdom, and the power, and the glory, now and forever, amen"*)

Pray the Our Father with me, and as we pray the Lord's Prayer—be it with our voices or in the silence of our hearts—let us pray with our whole being.

"Our Father"

***

Remember when I said the more I received, the more I wanted? This also holds true in reverse. The more God asks of us, the more He will ask of us and, yes, the more we will receive. This forgiveness thing, which has an effect on us and those around us, is all true! One of the most powerful gifts God gives to us is *forgiveness*. At the same time, this *forgiveness* is the very *gift* the devil wants to destroy in us. *When you feel cleansing going through you, healing starts to take place*, and the plan the devil has gets destroyed. The Lord will stand by you as He promised.

Listen to these words from Jesus. He came to me in this song, as He does in all my songs, but they are not mine. They are His and for His people. He does not give to me for me to keep but to share with you. He gives to you. Listen. He is speaking to us right now in this song. In this song, He is telling us He stands with us. He wants us to follow him, and He tells us He is waiting for us. He's waiting for you and me right now.

"Stand by You"

***

Jesus will always stand by you. You are His own.

Forgiveness is powerful—the cleansing, the healing, the setting free of ourselves from the devil who wants to bind us to our sinfulness—but instead, we hold fast to the promise of God. Jesus will always stand by us! Amen!

Healing

I remember one day, in the middle afternoon, as I was holding on to these teachings, I knew what else I had to do. I should mention that moments earlier, Neil pulled his back out and was in a lot of pain. I told my children to come upstairs with me to pray over their dad for his back to be healed, but getting their father to go upstairs and lie on the bed to be prayed over was a challenge. Not that he didn't believe in God, but this praying over people was something of which he was quite sure he did not want any part. However, when he saw his children kneeling down by the bed waiting to pray over him, he said okay. The three of us prayed with conviction, and the Lord heard our faithful cries and healed their father. Neil got up from the bed and could not understand what he was witnessing. The pain was gone. He could walk and climb the stairs with no effort. He was indeed healed. Praise God! Hallelujah! Amen!

Once after a special retreat during my morning prayer, I was asked to make a phone call to Danny and his mom who lived in Rhode Island. I lived in Connecticut. We were strapped for money, and back then, phone calls were very expensive. I remember only thinking, "Oh Lord, that's long distance."

But then I heard in my thoughts His soft voice say to me, "My daughter, dial only the seven digits. The call will go through."

I did as asked and the call went through just as I was told. God is so good!

Another time, my eleven-year-old daughter and I were coming home from a church concert by the Celebrant Singers. As we traveled on this half-dirt, lonely road I noticed lights in the far distant right. The lights had me reflecting on the dream I had the night before. I was traveling this same road with the same lights in the far distant right. As the two roads met, a car crashed into the right side of my car where my daughter Jennifer was sitting. As I remembered my dream, I realized this was another warning, so I slowed down to a stop and waited for the car to go by. We got home safely. Praise God!

Remember the teachings I was blessed in receiving about all the many ways God speaks to us? Well, for me, a very important way was also in my dreams. God gave me warning signs in my dreams. No, I did not know it at the time of my dream nor did I even remember my dream when I woke up, but on that day, and at the very instant needed, I remembered the dream and listened to my warning. God is not limited in the ways He speaks to you.

I remember dreaming of Rita, another cousin very dear to my heart. This time, when I woke, I remembered my dream, and I could not shake the feeling of the uncertainty of this dream. I knew something was wrong, but I didn't know what. I called her and found she needed prayers to help her deal with the loss of her mom who had died the night before. Now whenever I dream of someone I know, I pray for them because we never know why we dream of them. Prayers always help. It's a good practice to get into.

Another time, I was on retreat, and during a teaching I found hard to understand, I got up and went outside for some air and to be alone with God. It was evening, but the moon gave me light, so I sat on the steps and prayed. I remembered asking God, "Lord, if you want me to go back to that teaching, please give me a sign." He did. A skunk came to me, crawled under my legs over my arms, and sniffed at my face. As I held my breath, I silently prayed, "Okay, Lord, I hear you. I'll go back in." The skunk gently left me, and I returned to the teaching unharmed.

I can go on and on and on. There is just no end to what God can do when we let Him in our lives. Praise God!

One day, when I was babysitting for my dear friend Gwen, I was in prayer and heard that sweet soft voice speak these words to me in my thoughts: "You will minister in songs on many far lands you have not yet walked. You will speak my words, for my Spirit will lead you. You will not stay long in one place, and I will lead your travels. I will be with you. Will you follow me, my daughter?"

Will I follow the Lord who is calling me? I cried tears of joy to the Lord and said YES to God's calling!

I asked the Lord to confirm this (as Sister Bern taught me to do), and the Bible verses He gave me were:

> The Spirit of the Lord will control you, you will prophesy with them and you will be transformed into a different person. When these signs have happened to you, do whatever your circumstances require because God is with you. (1 Sam. 10:6–7)
>
> Pay attention to the ministry you have received in the Lord so that you can accomplish it. (Col. 4:17)

I believe the Lord my God was truly preparing me, one step at a time, little by little, for this journey ahead. I shared my journal with my spiritual directors. They prayed, and I received confirmations. My life as I knew it was already changing and the choices were becoming harder and more difficult. Still, I knew it was a journey I had to make.

I prayed and offered up my children to God, and He said to me, "Because you have heard my voice and answered my call, your children are saved. No evil can claim them. They are mine. But you, my daughter, will receive a mother's worst separation, and you will suffer much rejection. Are you willing to suffer for my will and follow me?"

"I am, Lord. Use me as you will, not my will. I desire only your will, Lord, to be done in me. I love you, Lord. Amen." This was my prayer.

The following day, as I was praying, I realized the Lord was preparing me in ways that all I could see in front of me was a journey of uncertainties. As I listened, I heard these words within my thoughts concerning my husband: "When he comes home today, he will come to you with three choices. You are not to choose. He must do the choosing, then abide by his choice."

It happened as I was told. Neil got home and came to me with his three choices: the first was separation within the house, the second was separation outside the house, and the third was divorce. I abided by his choice, but I could not believe in my heart a divorce was in my future, especially since I still loved him. It felt like it was a bad dream. If it were not for the grace and mercy of God, the Holy Spirit leading me into truth, and this personal relationship in Jesus, then I may never have experienced *healing* and true *joy* in *suffering*.

I was blessed in becoming more aware of God's ways. I found the more I gave of my time, the more time was given me. The more I listened, the more I would hear. The more I heard and obeyed, the more was asked of me. Everything I have experienced have in no way been *co-incidences*; they have all have been *God-incidences.* Sister Bern and Father Bill would say this all the time, and it's true. I was having a personal relationship with Jesus. He opened my mind, my eyes, my ears, and my whole being through the power of His Holy Spirit. Living in the Spirit is a very powerful gift. I cannot survive without the Father, Jesus, and the Holy Spirit. Only through the grace and mercy of our mighty God have all these things been done. I can't even pray nor can I breathe a single breath without God's grace and mercy. This is why I live life in the Spirit. For me, there is no turning back.

Johnny turned thirteen in September 1984. It was a new chapter in his life and in his sister's life.

Life as they knew it would never be the same. *Divorce* affects everyone in a family. It is not easy, not wanted, yet as much as it broke my heart, it did take place. In fact, all the Lord revealed to me was coming to light.

I must always keep the words of God concerning my children close to my heart, for with all my heart, my soul, and my being, I trust in the Lord completely forever and always!

I must also keep in mind God will never forsake me. He is with me always, and though it may seem hard at times, I must keep my eyes focused on He who has called me to Himself. I will praise Him always. The Lord will open my lips, and I will praise His holy name forever. Amen.

Fifteen-Year Mission

It was a new chapter in my life, which included a ministry of worship, prayer, and music and everything else that will take place on my journey. What is the mission? To complete this part of my journey. But first, I needed to go to the church where my rosary beads were still on the cross with Jesus. It was time for my mission to begin with my prayer beads in my hand.

On the last week of November 1984, a strange manager/client type marriage between Delsie and me took place. It was performed by a justice of the peace, not the usual husband/wife marriage and a much different type of unity, but that was all my heart could agree to. There would be no doubt this journey was going to be a long and hard road. It would last for fifteen years, but it was part of my journey. From November 1984 until May 1985, we lived in the deep woods of Colchester, Connecticut, in a little log cabin. I was given a choice of which room I could have, and my choice was the large beautiful loft overlooking the living room. I stayed in touch with Sister Bern and Father Bill and received much support through their prayers as I continued to seek God's will. Looking through the newspapers, checking out the maps, and praying about our next move took us into even deeper woods of tall pines standing high on the mountaintop of Pittsfield, New Hampshire. So the little log cabin was sold, and off we traveled into the unknown.

May 1985, Pittsfield, New Hampshire

The first thing we did with our fifteen-acre wooded lot on this mountain peak overlooking the nearby towns and lakes was to clear for a driveway one-tenth of a mile long.

Delsie bought me a small chainsaw, and that year, I learned how to cut down trees and clear land. We cleared one acre of wooded land. Then I learned how to build forms up for pouring a cement wall for our home. Now that too was interesting. Then came the concrete floor for our home because the first floor was half in the ground. There wasn't any cellar, not even a crawl space. This began our log home with its attached garage. We slept in the van until the roof of the house was up. From the back side, it looked like an A-frame chalet, but from the front, it was more like a small cottage-style log home. At the peak of our loft on the front side, we built a special cross glass window, which

can be seen for miles. It was so beautiful, especially when the loft lights were on at night. We also put in roof windows on both sides of the house so we could watch the sun rise and set. I really loved that little log home.

After our home was built, we, with one other couple, Doug and Patti, started a small contracting business. We went on to build their home and then on to other building jobs for homes, garages, roofing, and remodeling.

I remember one time when Delsie took the electric circular saw out of my hands while I was using it. It ran over my fingers, and I screamed and cried from the pain. I looked down as I held my hand tightly and prayed, "God, please help me." Then I slowly looked at my hands, but not a finger was hurt. The pain was so bad I could not believe how it could hurt so much, yet I was okay. All I could do was praise God. I knew somehow the Lord intervened. I just knew. God is so good!

There were times when I felt truly weak in my body. I needed to go off and just be by myself with the Lord. I remembered being on this lonely dirt road walking and praying. Far ahead of me, I noticed a woman letting her two large dogs out, and whatever she said to them made them come charging at me. Fearful for my life and remembering one of the teachings (from Father Bill and Sister Bern on authority) as both dogs leapt at me, I said with authority, "Stop in the name of the Father and of the Son and of the Holy Spirit, and go home!" They both fell to the ground facing me, turned around, and went back to the house they came from. Then I breathed again and said, "Thank you, Lord Jesus, heavenly Father, and Holy Spirit!" I praised God all the way home.

One weekend, I received a surprise visit. I was walking through the woods of our land and heard a car drive up our long dirt driveway. I looked to see who it could be and started running toward the car as fast as my feet could take me for God just gave me the gift I was longing for in my heart—my parents came to see me. They slept in our loft that weekend. We enjoyed each other so much as we played games and shared meals together. Then we parted and they went back home, but oh, how I wished they could stay longer.

After they left, the following day, I went into this little town of Pittsfield and found it quite interesting as I walked by a little white church overlooking the waterfall, walked by a popular family restaurant with an attached Laundromat. This little town seemed to have everything we needed. Later, I was blessed with a job waitressing at this popular family restaurant called Bell Bros. Restaurant where my boss, Ruthi, and I became good friends. She seemed to have noticed Delsie's ways and one day she went up to him, while he and I was sitting in a booth, and she said to him, 'you better treat this lady good.' He shyly smiled and said he would. But I wondered about that day, for I see Ruthi as an angel in my life and a good friend I will always remember.

I also became a music minister at this little white Catholic church called Our Lady of Lourdes. I took Bible classes and a course on the holy Eucharist. Then when my studies were done, Rev. Richard Giroux commissioned me as Eucharistic minister in March 1987. I was so blessed to serve at Our Lady of Lourdes Church.

I looked forward to the travels back and forth, being with my children, visiting my parents, and keeping in touch with Father Bill and Sister Bern for I needed their prayers so much.

After being in Pittsfield, New Hampshire, for nearly three years and really getting attached not only to Delsie's daughter, Lisa, and her little family but also all the people I served at my church, I knew a move was coming soon. I never got to try out my new antique wood and gas stove that stood so nicely in my kitchen or feel the warmth of the wood burning in the fireplace, but I did feel God's blessings on Lisa, her family, and all those people I was so blessed to serve. When we sold our home, we came back to stay a week or so at My Father's House Retreat Center with Father Bill and Sister Bern for guidance and prayers on our next move. My heart was longing to be part of their retreat, but I knew my journey wasn't there, though I did pray if it could be God's will for us to stay and still prayed for God's will to be done. God is so good, and I know He is with me always. After praying and discerning our next move, it was time to go, and we headed for Tennessee. Sister Bernadette told me to let her know when we got settled there, and she would arrange a meeting for me with June Carter Cash so I looked forward for that meeting to happen. Sister Bern was good friends with Johnny Cash and his wife. They often stayed at My Father's House Retreat Center for their retreats. It was a while before we got there, but finally, we arrived.

1988, Goodlettsville, Tennessee

We moved right into a trailer park. I did a lot of country and gospel singing. I was in a lot of shows and got to know a few producers. I thought it all was looking good for me, especially when I found myself singing in showcases and meeting up with Barbara Mandrell's lead rhythm guitarist, Stephen Preston, and his guitarist buddy, Randy Butler. They even backed me on one of my own songs, "Come and Take Me Away." For sure, I really thought I was doing okay, but I guess my manager, Delsie, had different ideas and just kept rejecting the offers that came my way. Of course I didn't know this until many years later. My brother always said I was naïve, and he was right. I trusted when I should have checked things out on my own. Instead, I had no idea what my manager was up to, and I had no idea what he was capable of doing. When Delsie told me the meeting with June Carter Cash had been canceled, I had no idea he was the one who canceled it. He told me they no longer wanted to meet with me. Then Delsie had us drive to a new place far from Tennessee.

1989, Beatrice, Nebraska

We started again on another fifteen-acre, but not a single tree—only a field of dreams. While building our small home, we again built a cross made of glass into the peak, which can be seen for miles, and I loved that cross. It was beautiful. I also loved the sweet town of Beatrice.

I became one of the music leaders for St. Joseph's Catholic Church with a girl I befriended named Pam who sang the best harmonies I ever heard. I was also doing country, opry, and gospel shows there. I had my own band plus was in other country bands and a great gospel band, which I loved most of all. The leader's name in the gospel band was Francine, and she and I became good friends. As in Francine's life, gospel and spiritual songs and sharing about God in my life made me come alive. However, there were warning signs that made me realize Delsie was becoming noticeably dangerous, and I knew I needed to leave. Yet he was like Dr. Dirks, finding me no matter where I would go. Before leaving this state, among the songs I wrote was this prayer that I cried out to the Lord so many times.

"Lead Me Lord"

***

Lead Me Lord is about me trying to do the Lord's will yet finding it so hard because no one understands—no one but God. Yet I knew God indeed would lead me through my journey. Still I cried that prayer many times throughout my journey, wondering if my life could have taken a different turn. I would be haunted by the uncertainties that still lay ahead and by past memories I left behind though I knew well I needed to move on, let go, and let God lead my life. I had to keep reminding myself God is with me, and He will always be with me. Jesus heard my prayer, and the Holy Spirit gave me strength to continue my journey.

February 1992, Nashville, Tennessee

I left Beatrice by myself (though not alone for long) and headed to Tennessee by way of Louisiana. However, even by way of Louisiana, Delsie still found me in Nashville, and within one month, we were in Savannah, Georgia, for a short stay. There, I would learn to keep quiet about my fears. One day, he followed my little car with his big van, and I guess I just wasn't moving fast enough for him. As we stopped at an intersection I must have stayed at too long, he pushed my car with his monster van across the lanes and toward the bridge we were heading for. I don't need to tell you how hard I prayed for God to save me that day. God did, and no one was hurt. We were there for just a couple of months, but those months gave me insight to how my life had to play out (almost like an old teaching written by a man—pray, pay, and obey— kind of gives new meaning to Delsie's twisted lessons).

I praised my Lord my God for it was only Him I trusted to lead me through this journey. I know this: God is good all the time!

May 1992, Lake City, South Carolina

I was blessed to sing and be the church music director of this little church, St. Phillip Catholic Church in Lake City, South Carolina, but let me tell you: talk about your history books. This here place was like walking right back into old history books.

On our first visit, we walked into the church and sat on the right side, about four pews from the front. As I waited in prayer for Mass to begin, a sweet little old lady came over to me and said, "My dear, you are sitting on the wrong side."

I said, "Oh, I'm sorry. Did I take your seat?"

She smiled and went off elsewhere. Then I felt a little tap on my shoulder, and I turned to the lady in back of me who said, "You may want to change sides."

I smiled at her and asked why. Do I have someone's seat? She just smiled and went back to reading her prayer book.

Now Mass was starting, and there was no music? So that made me think maybe I'll check with the priest after Mass to see if he would like me to lead in music. This made me hopeful. Then it was time for the sign of peace. The priest came over to us to give the sign of peace and welcome us. It was already feeling like home. As he continued back to the altar and we continued with the sign of peace, I noticed something strange. I had never seen this ever except maybe in history books from my grade school years. The church people on the left side were all white while the church people on the right side were all black. Well, except for Delsie and me. I could not believe what I was experiencing.

After going to Mass daily for two weeks and continuing to sit on the right side, people were coming over to me asking me why. I said, "Why not?"

Two Sundays later, the priest came over to me and asked if he could see us after church. We visited with him and a few nuns. They were so sweet. We even helped them in moving things from one house to another. Then they asked me if I had any music background, and I jumped for joy. I told them of my background and that I had my guitar and keyboard with me, and they made me their music minister right there on the spot. I couldn't have been happier. I'm not sure how the parishioners felt, but I did not allow that to sway my decisions.

Before each Sunday Mass, I would hand out my Mass music sheets and walk from the front to the back with guitar in hand, playing and teaching the music. When I wasn't playing, I would sit in my usual seat (the right side of the church), which according to many of the people there was the wrong side. Now when they came over to question me why, my answer was becoming obvious to them that Jesus was on both sides, so it didn't matter which side. Close to four or so months passed when they too were doing the same, sitting on either side. The priest allowed me to use the church to write my church and spiritual music and keep my keyboard in the back of the church. Our pastor even wanted me to write him his music (Mass) parts, and so I did. He loved it and loved having us there, I loved them all too. God is always so good! But keep in mind I am no stranger to the saying "all things must come to an end." How true that is.

We were getting our land ready for building our home when I picked up a cough I could not get rid of, and it gave me trouble breathing. It would happen every time we went out to our land. The doctor told me it was an allergy, but I didn't know what allergy I had. Then he asked us when it happened. He knew the area well and said the crops next door to our land were ready for picking. Then he told me it was the tobacco fields to which I was seriously allergic. Needless to say, we put our land back on the market and stayed elsewhere in walking distance of our church. Two years later, we moved on. I will never forget that little church in Lake City, South Carolina. So much has happened there in just two years. The Holy Spirit was so active in that place. People no longer sat only on one side; they sat and allowed the Holy Spirit to move them wherever the Spirit moved them. I loved being part of that, serving that beautiful parish and all the people there. I will miss that place so much, and I will always have all the people there in my heart of prayers, always and forever.

1995, Hope Hall, Alabama

Hope Hall was a short stay while we lived at a hotel where we worked. Delsie took care of the ground work while I worked at the front desk. I also did gospel concerts at our Lady Queen of Mercy Catholic

Church. While we were there, Delsie searched the maps and newspapers as we prayed for the Lord to lead us to our next move. We got a hold of a realtor in Troy, Alabama. He would show us homes in the nearby area, but I just wasn't feeling right about the places he was taking us to.

One day, as he took us on this long secondary highway about ten miles out, I prayed my heart's desire to the Lord, and my heart's prayer went like this: "Lord, can you find us a home on top of the highest peak overlooking the horizon for miles and miles, and can it be far from the road and have a fence and a gate and maybe a few peach trees on the front lawn? And can the house have a large warm sunroom with lots of windows to bring in the light where I can offer you my all and all my music? Lord, am I asking for too much?"

Then, while we were a few miles from where the realtor was taking us, I looked into the far distance up high and *instantly* knew that was where the Lord wanted us. I was looking at my soon-to-be home. So I said to the realtor, "You're taking us to that house on the top of the peak there."

He pulled over to the side of the road and said, "How did you know?"

With my happy eyes, I said, "I just do." Then he continued driving.

As we pulled into the driveway, I could see flowers on the front side of the house and a few beautiful little peach trees on the front lawn with a fence and a gate to get into the backyard of the house. This house stood high on the highest peak overlooking the horizon for miles and miles. I was in awe of the Lord and what He can do and does for me. The realtor took us through the house from the back side. The backyard had extras—a barn and a large L-shape in-ground swimming pool. There were two doors in the back and one in the front, going to a closed-in porch with windows on three sides. The fourth door was on the front end of the house, going into, *yes*, the most beautiful sunroom I've ever seen. It took my breath away. Praise you, Lord, forever and always. God is so good!

The realtor then took us to town to talk business, and I got to tell you: that realtor had never experienced, in all his days, what he saw was happening. I think if he wasn't, he sure became a believer in God that day!

He took us to his office and told us the price. Ninety-five thousand dollars, he said.

Delsie looked at me, and I said, "No, that don't seem right."

The realtor said, "I'll be back," and he stepped out to talk with the seller on the phone. Then he came back in and said, "I'm sure I can get her to drop it some, so why don't you talk it over and tell me what you'd like to offer."

I had been praying about it, and I know Delsie trusted the Lord in my prayers. When I heard the Lord tell me what to offer, I looked at Delsie and said softly, "I just heard the Lord tell me, 'Offer $57,953, my little one. Do not go higher or lower. When my daughter hears this offer, she will agree.'"

All I could do was what I heard my Lord tell me, and I said to God, "Your will be done, Lord. Amen."

The realtor came back in, and Delsie said to him, "We'd like you to offer her $57,953."

The realtor said, "She's not going to accept that, and how did you come up with that figure?"

I told him that was what I heard in my prayer from God.

He said, "$57,953.00?"

I said, "Yes"

He sat down for a moment; guess he didn't know what to do with that. Then he said, "Okay, I'll go offer her that, but I'm sure she will not take that offer."

I said, "You need to offer it to her because it is the only offer we are making."

It took him a little longer to return this time, but when he did, he sat down and said, "I can't believe it. I cannot believe she said what she said. She took your offer. She asked your name, and I told her Sheila. She said she believes the Lord sent you, and the house is meant for you. But she also said she wanted you to know the couple who owned the house before her got divorced while living there, and she also got a divorce while living in that house so beware." I asked him for her name, and he said, "Her name is yours. Her name is Sheila."

All I could say was God's will was done that day. We listened and followed His will, and the rest was out of our control and in God's hands. God is so good! Praise God forever! Amen.

February 1996, Elba, Alabama

We moved into our home. Our church was in Enterprise, Alabama. I was blessed again with a commitment as a minister of the Eucharist and music minister for St. John Catholic Church. God has blessed me over and over, and I just can't tell you of the many blessings God has put into my life.

I was blessed to be able to plan an event with Sister Bernadette and Father Bill for my parent's fiftieth wedding anniversary on October 19, 1996. They renewed their vows at a special Mass held at My Father's House Retreat Center in Moodus, officiated by our special Rev. Bill McCarthy and followed by a dinner given in our parent's honor by their children. Our parents are truly a very special blessing! Praise the Lord forever and always! God is so good!

Oh, how I hated to leave, but my journey was not over.

Back in Elba, Alabama, where my music was spreading wide into Florida. I had years of doing spiritual country and gospel music at local parks, churches, retreat shows, and opry shows. The church leaders of St. John's Catholic church and I became good friends. I truly found a sort of comfort and safety there. The pastor and the church people seemed to have wisdom in their ways and thoughts. They also seemed to have Delsie figured out and seemed to be concerned and protective of me. I knew the Lord was doing something there, but I just didn't know what yet.

Remember my Elba home known for its divorces?

December of 1998, while living in the Alabama home, Delsie and I were divorced from our strange manager/client type marriage. We sold our home and moved into the town of Enterprise near our church where I could receive support from my church people there. Being able to serve in that parish has given me hope, and I will never forget all the people there. I have received so much more than I had given and more blessings than I ever could have dreamed. God's people are everywhere working and doing His will.

You may not know it, but the one you befriend may be one of God's special angels put into your life just for you, just as all those people who were put into my life just for me. God is so good always. So good.

February 1999, Enterprise, Alabama

There was a plan in the making, and that plan was to get me back home to Connecticut in one piece. The church people, the priest, and the clergy all had a part in this plan, and this is what happened one Sunday at Mass. Father Hugh Maguire announced I was taking leave from the music leadership and returning back to Connecticut to care for my mom. I was on the altar with Father Maguire and Delsie was in the front pew, so he had no way of pulling me out of church. Father told everyone that day was my last, I would be leaving the following morning to go back home to Connecticut, and if anyone wished to see me, to please just come up onto the altar right after Mass. I could not believe that was happening. I had no idea about what they all were doing. I was so deeply touched by all that was being done just for me.

As each and every person hugged me with their best wishes and prayers, I cried my thanks to them and the Lord. Delsie was walked out of the church by our Father Maguire. In the morning, one of my friends came over to see me off while several of the church people stayed close by the apartment to make sure Delsie would not follow me or try to stop me from leaving.

I remember, while on the highway back home, I would check my rearview mirror often. When I needed to rest, I would pull over into a truck stop where there were lots of people. Through prayers lots of prayers and the help of Father Maguire, my friend Mary, and all my church friends, God was bringing me home. This part of my journey was bringing me back to more familiar surroundings.

That fifteen-year mission was now over. God was bringing me to a haven in Connecticut, and I will praise His holy name forever!

Thank you, Father, for your unconditional love. Thank you, Jesus. You died that I may have life more abundantly, and thank you, Holy Spirit, for leading me and empowering me in my being! Amen.

Haven in Connecticut

February 1999, New Britain, Connecticut

Yes, the fifteen-year mission was now over, and the ministry part of my journey was slowing down. I needed time to care for my mom and dad and reconnect with family and friends. I also needed time to meditate and recuperate from the many places I traveled in my one nation under God.

I stayed with my parents until my next move. I needed *time-out* to just *breathe* again, but it wasn't for long (my mom didn't believe in *time-outs*).

It was only after one week of being home when I found myself working at a printing place, which was not something I wanted. However, my mom had a different idea. In trying to help me, without my knowledge, my mom asked my brother to get me a job where he was working. He did, and I worked there for less than a year, but working there had its own purpose—again, not to my knowledge but also not to my mom's knowledge either. I believe God's plan was at work there for that was where I met John. My mom then took me to her hairdresser's studio where I could get my hair done. I met an excellent beautician name Jeannine, and we became very good friends. (Do you see the pattern here? Who said fathers know best? Shouldn't it be mothers know best? Hmm.)

I had many conversations with the Lord in my prayers concerning John. I didn't yet understand this plan and wasn't sure if I wanted to be part of it, yet more than life itself, I knew I wanted God's will done in me and in my life. Not my will; only God's will.

One night, I prayed, "Lord, how about just you and me?"

Next day at work, John talked more to me. My brother visited my station and also talked to me about John. I asked him what he really thought of John, and his answer was plain and simple. He's a good man, he said. He wears cowboy boots, so he must be a good man. Not really what I wanted to hear just getting back home from a cowboy boot–type of life.

That night, in my prayers, I asked God, "Lord, if you want John in my life, he needs to be Catholic."

The next day at work, while sitting by myself in the lunchroom, John came over and sat with me. In our conversation John shared with me that he is Catholic and was wondering what I was.

Wow, Lord, now that was a fast answer! Still, I am not sure, so that night, in prayer, I said, "Okay, Lord, he's Catholic, but is he spiritual?"

Next day at work, John came up to me, and in our conversation, shared with me he is a spiritual person and goes to Mass every Sunday.

You know where this is going, right? I was having this personal relationship with the Lord, and I do not, in any way, want to give that up—and I won't, not *ever!* So back on my knees, in my conversations with God, I said, "Lord, are you saying you want John in my life?"

Then I heard the soft voice of my Lord say to me, in my thoughts, "Yes, my daughter, I do. This is part of my plan."

"Okay," I said. "Your will be done, Lord. I love you, my Lord. I trust completely in you, Lord. I love you. Amen." Then I went to sleep in God's love.

God has so much to do. To think He would put so much thought about me; He loves me that much! He loves you that much too! God is love. Just think about that. God loves us so much, you and me, that He desires and waits for us to talk with Him in our hearts and keeps loving us unconditionally. God is love! I was always finding myself in awe of God, no matter how many times or how many ways God always answers my prayers. I may not, at times, perceive His answers, but always He answers my prayers. God is so good!

2002, Middletown, Connecticut

This is where my next move took place. My brother and John helped me move into my own little condominium. At the time, I was at a different job and driving a company truck. My new home was near my job and not far from my parents and My Father's House Retreat Center, both of which I liked. I also started singing country at places where Jeannine would take me. Then I found different local places in Middletown to sing some blues and folk music while my own ministry was waiting for me to sing of the Lord's praises.

For reasons unknown to me, I was feeling my spiritual music being pretty much rejected, and I didn't know how to get it started up again. I visited My Father's House Retreat Center but didn't get to

spend any time with Sister Bern or Father Bill for my timing these days was off, and they were doing missions. I was feeling a sense of loss, like I was missing the depth of my prayer life. Country and blues just didn't do it for me. Where's my Jesus in my life? Where's my life in the Spirit? Where's my personal relationship in Jesus? On my knees, I found myself praying, "Jesus, please help me. I need my personal relationship life in you. I need you! I need you, Lord. You are my life!"

May 2004

John and I were spending more time, sharing our lives together and becoming closer to each other.

Then one day, on our own separate journey and after I had been praying on the Lord's will in my own life, it became time for my brother Howard and John to move me into a home I called "my haven in Connecticut." It had been five years since John and I met, and now the Lord was blessing us into a purely beautiful relationship. He said, "I, have blessed you and John as soul mates, live in my peace and love." God, through His mercy and grace, even through all my imperfections, had prepared this haven for me, and He also prepared the heart of John to accept me as I am and open his home and heart to me. God is so good. God's love and peace abide here. God is with us. Holy and mighty is His name. Holy and mighty is our God. Thank you, Lord Jesus. Praise you, Lord, forever and always.

Now this is where my ministry picked up and became alive in me again. I started writing and recording again. I was having my personal relationship with Jesus that I felt I lost but never really lost. It was just a dry area in my life, making me feel my personal relationship with Jesus was gone, and that was the worst feeling I could ever feel. I cannot live without that personal relationship with the Father, Jesus, and the Holy Spirit in my life!

I went to reconnect again with Father Bill and Sister Bernadette and soon found myself deeply back into my prayer life and my ministry of music and prayer. My Father's House was always my second home; a place I could receive the spiritual help I counted on from my own spiritual directors.

I also continued spending as much time as I could with my mom and dad. I was enjoying the blessings of just doing things with them, like bringing them to their dance shows. My mom was so light on her feet with her tiny dancing shoes. "There she is," they would say, "the beautiful dancing Barbie doll," as she and my dad danced across the floor. But then one day, my mom took a bad fall on December 17, 2006. My mom and dad, with their dance team, were giving a most beautiful square and round dancing show I was blessed to see, and I'm so glad I videotaped them for it would be my mom's last show.

I lived with her fall, haunting at me. I should have been able to catch her, or I should not have stepped out in front of her when we were on that one last step down from the staircase ... I'm sure you know those feelings that I, at times, would torture myself with. It never stops hurting, but I know and I believed God would get us through all that life brings us and He will always be with us. Still, sometimes, life just hurts.

I joined an awesome group of people in their folk group in 2007, and the director, Huguette, and I became very close sisters in Christ and singing part-

ners at our church, St. Francis of Assisi in New Britain, Connecticut. Huguette also introduced me to a family of the Secular Franciscan Order (SFO) of St. Mary Frances of the Five Wounds of Jesus, and in August 2012, I became a member of  their SFO. At this time, I also joined another special choir from Holy Family Retreat, and truly, this fine director and deeply talented priest, Fr. David Cinquegrani, C.P. should be applauded for all his good works. While in the choir, I befriended another very special sister in Christ, and her name is Lonni.

She and I will very often enjoy the prayerful teachings and dinners given at her own church each month.

As I continued longing for more spiritual charismatic prayer in my life, I met yet another beautiful sister in Christ, Elizabeth, who truly seeks the will of God and the Holy Spirit's leading. She introduced me to their charismatic prayer group, which has been so fulfilling in my life and a place where the Holy Spirit truly is in control. Praise God! God is so good.

By this time, my own ministry was alive and well active once more with spiritual music and prayers. I never will forget the concert in September 2013 at My Father's House Retreat Center. I had to go early, and Huguette came with me. In fact, she was singing the opening song with me, the Hail Mary Prayer. John picked up my mom and dad and took them to the concert. Little did I know this would be the last concert my mom would attend.

On January 23, 2014, my mom wasn't feeling well, so my dad and I took her to see her doctor who admitted her into the hospital. She was suffering from heart failure. She started to do better, so on January 31, my mom was transferred to Jerome Home where she was expected to regain her strength so we could bring her home. She asked me to play her the music chaplet rosary prayers from my iPod, so I went home and put my divine mercy chaplet music and prayers on the iPod, took it back with me, and placed it under her pillow where she could listen to it as she slept and as often as she liked. She loved it, and I was so happy she did. As time went on, her condition changed for the worse, and on February 19, she was placed in hospice care.

On February 22, 2014, around five in the morning, while my dad was sleeping near my mom's bedside in the recliner, I got up from where I was sleeping at the foot of my mom's bed in another recliner, and I went to talk to her. As I was looking at my beautiful mom, she opened her eyes, looked into my face, and said hi with the most beautiful, peaceful love in her smile I ever saw. Then she closed her eyes, and I went back to the recliner. To this day, I'm still not sure if my mom was really looking at me or if she just experienced someone from the other side waiting to take her home. At six o'clock, I saw my mom take her last breath. I know the joy she received. I saw it on her face and felt it in her ever sweet hi. But my dad just lost the love of his life, and this new chapter was going to be hard on him. My brother and I tried to no end to make his life happy, but we could not keep his heart from breaking.

We drove him to places and to his appointments, but one day, he left before I got to his home. At first, we couldn't find him. Then we found him and found out he was in a small accident, which totaled his car, but no one was hurt. Praise God. So no car for my dad right now, but he sure wanted his car back. We all talked him into getting a dog, but by November 2014, his dog, Jessie, passed away. The sadness seemed to be multiplying. Now my dad grew even more determined in getting himself another Ford Focus. His doctor told him he's better off not driving but would not sign anything that would take his driver's license away. There really wasn't any way of denying him his rights, so another car he got and he proudly drove his Ford Focus.

Now my brother's body was also failing him and his condition was getting worse and he was placed on hospice care. Howie left his earthly body a little past midnight on January 17, 2015. Chronic obstructive pulmonary disease robbed him of a longer life and robbed me of having my brother longer, but my poor dad, how empty his heart must have been. First, his wife who was the love of his life, then Jessie his dog that he loved, and now his only son is gone. I constantly found myself praying, "I need your help, Lord, in helping my dad. Please help me be the daughter he needs. Let not his heart hurt him so much."

I continued to be with him even more, and I took him with me everywhere. He enjoyed going to all the concerts I was giving and enjoyed just being with us. Still, his losses took a big part out of him, and no matter how much he tried, that hole in his heart was too great. This little man was very healthy, but nothing can cure a broken heart. All I can do, all anyone of us can do, is our best, and let God do the rest. I know in my heart only God can heal my dad's broken heart, and forever my trust is in the Lord. I continued to pray for God's holy will to be done for my dad and in my dad's life. God is good, and forever and always, I will trust in my God! Amen.

Transformation

May 15, 2016, Pentecost Sunday

A smooth transformation was taking place now. My last concert was being given. It marked the end of one chapter and the beginning of a new chapter. Through the grace and mercy of God, my journey continues. I have gone from a ministry of giving only concerts to a ministry as an evangelist witness speaker while still using the music God has given me as a tool. With the breath of God and fire within, I do not walk alone but with Him who calls me to Himself.

This is where I am in my life.

A calling I hear but one I am unfamiliar with. Still, if He who knows me with all my faults and limited knowledge has called me into this new chapter,

He who has brought me through all these other chapters of my journey, then I must say, "Yes, Lord!" For only through the grace and mercy of God can I, a poor sinner, pray yes with our Blessed Mary's prayer and have a personal relationship with the very breath of God, with Jesus!

> My sheep hear My voice, I know them, and they follow Me. (John 10:27)

I live by this scripture, and I can live no other way. I follow His voice because He makes all things possible. He brings my darkest nights into everlasting light. Through His mercy and grace, He forgives my sins and brings me to Himself. He is *life*! If nothing more than this, I pray you who are reading this book or listening to my testimony right now, please pay close attention to your inner self, to your surroundings, to His soft voice within your very own thoughts, and to your dreams. God is not limited. He speaks to each one of us differently and in ways all around us. God works in you and through you. *See with God's eyes His miracles in you.*

At this time, I like to pray this song prayer I wrote for the Lord called "I Am Yours." It's my "surrendering prayer to the Father, Son, and Holy Spirit," which was composed in 1981. As with all surrendering prayers, it helps me reach deep into the center of God's blessings. It's a simple, heartfelt prayer. It is the giving of oneself to the Father, to Jesus, and to the Holy Spirit.

"I Am Yours"

***

This chapter took place on the weekend of Pentecost Sunday on May 15, 2016. A Holy Spirit concert was given on Sunday at My Father's House Retreat Center in Moodus, Connecticut. However, the day I am speaking of is the Saturday before. I drove there to set up my gear and prepare for the concert. I was no stranger to this task as it had been my way of life since my teen years. Although something was off and I was unaware of what it was, I somewhat knew this feeling for I have gone through it many times before, yet I could not touch it with clarity. When I got there, I needed to wait until the room where I would be setting up was ready for me to use, so I waited in the chapel. "What better place to be," was my thought. There I was, alone with God and my thoughts. "If only I could shake this feeling," I thought, then I would feel better, but that did not happen.

My being was instead taken to a very cold and dark place of uncertainties. I could feel my heart filling with tears as the feeling of mourning took possession of my being. I had this overwhelming sense this was going to be my last concert. So many feelings and thoughts were attacking my mind and going in all different directions, yet understood only that something was happening. I was shaken with the knowledge of knowing something is changing, and part of my journey would soon be over. "Tomorrow is the last page," was my thought.

"But what, Lord? Oh Lord, my God, why can't I hear you? You are stirring in me something so strong. Tell me, Lord. Are you taking me home? I want to do your will, Lord. You know I do. I love you, my Lord. You are my life …"

Then I took a breath and said, "Amen."

One hour and twenty-five minutes of unbearable darkness, and now it was time for me to set-up.

Though set-up took only fifteen minutes or less, it felt like an eternity. It seemed to have taken every breath I had to continue. I finished, and now it was time for my forty-minute drive back home. On my drive there, I had the Rosary CD on, but on the way back home, I prayed for God's mercy with my divine mercy chaplet.

Okay, I'm home, but what now? I don't even remember my drive home. I must have been in auto-pilot. What do I do now? I walked in and saw John, which usually makes me smile, only this time, I didn't know what I was feeling. My usual hi was replaced with an unprepared thought that came forth from my mouth: "I need to downsize." Now why would I say that? What did that even mean? I walked across the kitchen into the living room and sat down, but who was that really walking? It was as though all my thoughts and movements were also in autopilot. I was broken on the inside. All I could do was to be in silence. I prayed, "Your will, Lord. Your will be done in me." Then I took a breath and said, "Amen."

The next day, it was Pentecost Sunday. I'm able to function but as to what degree was still question-able. I knew where I was supposed to be. I'm not a stranger to stepping out into the unknown. If I know nothing else, I know this: my complete trust is in Him who was calling me there. Trust in me? *Never*. But trust in God? *Always and forever!* So off I went.

There was a Pentecost Sunday Mass Service with Fr. Bill McCarthy, then followed by the concert. But what about this concert?

My body was no longer fighting, and it seems to be somewhat relaxing. Mass service is over and then it happened. The concert was given, and a transformation was taking place right before my very eyes. I felt on fire, and the dark place my soul was in was over taken by this "fire within"! Everything was clear!

I could see God's works. I could feel God's holy breath breathing on me. I could hear the soft voice of Jesus in my thoughts again. I was on fire again. I had "fire within" me, and I could not keep it silenced! That very moment, I felt the Holy Spirit taking control! The breath of God filled the room from the very first song.

"Holy Spirit Breath of God"

***

Now I knew my journey was moving into a new chapter. This truly was a smooth transformation without any separation. I knew this Pentecost day marked the last page of the chapter of worship prayer and music ministry I've known most of my life, yet at that very same moment, it became the first page of this new chapter. Through the mercy and grace of God, this fire within me began with the very breath of God. It began with saying yes to God's calling!

I know some of you have asked me how I can give up singing. I can't! I'm not! Singing is part of who I am and the me God made. Our heavenly Father gives His children many gifts. He gives to one teaching, another carpentry, another nursing, and the list is endless. One of the gifts God gave me was singing and writing. My yes to God is not giving up singing or writing, but rather it is using my singing and writing as a tool in this new ministry in which the Holy Spirit has called me. My yes to the Lord does not take away who I am; it doesn't take away His gifts. God doesn't give gifts so as to take them back from us. If we do not use the gifts God gives us, we may lose them, but it is not God taking them back. It is a choice we ourselves make.

I have gone from a ministry of giving only concerts to a ministry of giving witnesses that will still be using the music God has given me as a tool for this new chapter in my ministry. I knew now what that statement I heard my mouth speak was all about when I said, "I need to downsize." It became clear to me. It was making room for this new chapter in my journey. We all have different gifts and different journeys. My journey is different from yours. Yours is different from mine and everyone else. They all intertwine and complement each other's lives, but they are all different and your very own personal journey at that. He hears our prayers. He answers our prayers. We may not always be aware of His answer, as with me on that Saturday before Pentecost, but if we are faithful and hold on to His promise, He will answer us in ways that help us know we hear His soft voice within us. He speaks to each of us in ways we understand. He knows us! Believe it. He does speak to each of us in ways we understand. He knows us!

In the middle of December of this same year, God put in my heart a desire I didn't think possible. Then God granted it with His blessings, and I took my "vow of celibacy," making my relationship with John complete in Christ on the fourth Sunday of Advent in 2016 (which I've included at the end of this chapter).

As the holy gospel tells us in John 10:27: "My sheep hear My voice, I know them, and they follow Me."

I encourage you all as you pray your daily prayers and read Bible verses to also keep a spiritual journal of your quiet time with the Lord. He wants to bring you to Himself. He wants a personal relationship with you! Keeping a spiritual journal has helped me see my growth, my weaknesses, and my strengths. It has also made my relationship with Jesus deeper than I ever dreamed possible. God is so good!

*****

Stop here a moment with pen in hand, sit back in your chair, and rest in Jesus. Listen ... Now write your thoughts on the next page. It may be the voice of Jesus you hear in your thoughts. Jesus loves you ...

Keep this as the beginning of your Spiritual Journal with Jesus or as your continued Spiritual Journal with Jesus.

Spiritual journal with God...

We belong to Him who calls us to Himself! Jesus is calling you to Himself. Believe it in your whole being! Let the Holy Spirit breathe on you!

Say this with me:

Breathe on me, oh breath of God, and
make your presence known.
Thank you Holy Spirit! Amen? Amen!
So be it! So be it! Amen!
Living in the Spirit is my life for life! Amen.

Act of Consecration Prayer
Vow of Celibacy

December 18, 2016, the fourth
Sunday of Advent, 1:30 p.m.
Mass: My Father's House Chapel
Presiding priest: Fr. Bill McCarthy, MSA

*Written in obedience to my spiritual father, Fr. Bill
McCarthy, MSA, on December 17, 2016, 3:00 p.m.
Act of Consecration Prayer for my Vow of Celibacy*

Oh, my Jesus, I, Sheila S. Ward, make my Act of
Consecration to you in the presence of all here. I come
to you as I am in my nothingness—a sinner, a poor
and lowly servant—to give and consecrate all of me,
all I am, and all I have to you, Lord Jesus. My being
and everything belongs to you. I am only your servant, a vessel, and I deeply desire to take this vow of

celibacy. I long to say my yes with you, my Blessed Mary, to your holy son Jesus forever and always.

Help me, my Blessed Mother, to be obedient to the will of God as you are obedient to God's will.

Lord Jesus, through your mercy and grace, and through the powers of your Holy Spirit, I ask you, please take from me all that displeases you and fill me with only what is pleasing to you that I may be all I can be for your glory, oh God, giving you all glory, honor, and praise until you take me home and continue after my death.

I desire only your will in me, Lord. Not mine but your will alone to be done in me. I love you. Amen.

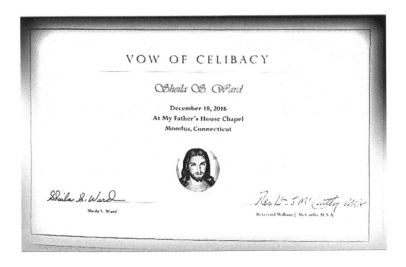

God Answers Prayers

My music transformation has opened doors into sharing and spreading the Word of God, God's wisdom, and new life in the Spirit seminars and speaking engagements.

I've been engaged into a deeper relationship with the Father who loves me, with Jesus who gave up His life that I may have life to the fullest, and with the Holy Spirit who forever empowers me in fulfilling God's will in my life. Praise His holy name forever and always!

It has also given me more time to spend with my dad, and now that he lost his driver's license, he was not a happy camper. But I really cannot say this enough: God is good. He answered my prayer about my ninety-three-year-young dad concerning his driving.

Now this new chapter for my dad has filled his life with so many new friends—our Mayor Erin E. Stewart (his first paper girl), Chief James P. Wardwell,

Lieutenant Benjamin M. Murphy, all of the police department of New Britain, the VA department, and many good neighbors and friends.

All who knew my dad was blessed by the many letters that would fill their keep sake places. He would brag about each and every one of his friends every chance he got. He was so very blessed, and I thank the Lord for them all. They blessed my dad's life with so much joy.

My dad was made the 2017 City of New Britain Memorial Day parade's grand marshal, but that was the day he fell sick and went into the Newington VA hospital. They transferred him to the West Haven VA, and in June (week of Father's Day), they transferred him to Autumn Lake in New Britain for rehab where he showed improvement. In July, however, his improvements came to a halt.

On July 14, Friday, at about five in the afternoon, I was sitting by his side on his bed when he turned to me with a glow beaming lovingly over his face and said, "Sheila, that house I have is yours now. I won't be needing it anymore." Then he turned his head back to whatever he was looking at and then again, he turned to me and said, "Sheila, that house I have is yours now.

I won't be needing it anymore." He did this one more time, only this last time, he also said, "You don't have to worry about me now. Go home, and get some rest."

I have never seen him in so much beauty of peace and love that just surrounded him completely. I wanted to ask, "Who do you see, Dad? But I was afraid he might lose that special heavenly joy he was experiencing.

Those were his last words to me. When we went to see him the following day, on July 15, the nurse shared with us about his last moment. My dad looked at her, smiled, and said, "I'm going home now," then closed his eyes. He left this world with so much joy, so much love, and so much peace.

I love you, Dad, and I will miss you, but oh, how happy I am for you.

Now in making the arrangements as my dad willed, the funeral was held in Maine. The night before his funeral, I prayed, "Please, Lord, bring my dad's buddy, the Lieutenant, here to see him off. Please, but your will be done, Lord. I love you, Lord. Amen."

The next morning, at the funeral home, who walks in but Lieutenant Ben from the New Britain police department.

Lord, you answered my prayer, and you touch my soul so deeply I could barely speak. Thank you, Lord Jesus. Lord, bless Lieutenant Ben with all your many blessings. How can I ever say thank you enough to you, Lord, and how can I ever thank the Lieutenant enough for answering your call to him to be here for my dad and carrying my dad to your altar in the church funeral liturgy service.

God is so good always and forever, God is good. Amen.

Does God answer prayers?

Does God care about all our concerns?

Is God good?

Yes!

Yes!

Yes!

God does answer prayers.

God cares about all your concerns.

God is good always and forever,

and God loves you so much!

See why I live life in the Spirit?

Living in the Spirit is my life for life! Amen.

My Morning Prayers

"My Morning Prayers" is my tiny chapter of prayers and part of my morning "ritual," with the first prayer being in remembrance to my mom, my dad, my brother, and my special spiritual director/mother, sister, and friend.

Sister Bernadette Sheldon, SCJ, 1932–2007
Mom, July 18, 1921–February 22, 2014
Howard, January 3, 1948–January 17, 2015
Dad, December 30, 1922–July 15, 2017

Rising Prayer

(I begin with an invitatory from the Office of Readings)

"Lord, open my lips, and my mouth
will proclaim your praise.
Glory to the Father and to the Son and to
the Holy Spirit, as it was in the beginning,
is now, and will be forever. Amen."

Good morning, heavenly Father. Thank you for this beautiful day. Good morning, merciful Jesus. Good morning, precious Holy Spirit. Good morning, beautiful Blessed Mother Mary. Good morning, all you angels and saints.

Good morning, my beautiful mom, my first hero dad, my gentle brother, and my spiritual mother. I sure do miss you all so much. Thank you, Father, for bringing these beautiful special saints into your heavenly kingdom and keeping them in your loving arms.

Thank you, Lord, for keeping all my loved ones here on earth in your loving arms and for all my blessings with which you have abundantly filled my life.

I love you so much, Lord. Breathe on me your divine will. Amen.

In Your Magnificat

I love you, my most Blessed Mother Mary, so deeply. I want to love you more and more and more. Help me be holy with a willing spirit to proclaim with you, Blessed Mary, in your Magnificat! I know I can never measure to even a tiny speck of your holiness, but I long to be holy as you are holy. I long to say my yes with you, my Blessed Mary, to your holy son Jesus forever and always. Help me, my Blessed Mother, to be obedient to the will of God, as you are obedient to His will. Help me, my Blessed Mary, to proclaim with you in your Magnificat. Amen.

Act of Consecration Prayer

My sweet Jesus, through your most sacred heart, through the immaculate heart of Mary, and through your divine mercy and grace, I trust in you. I give and consecrate everything to you—my life, my children, my loved ones. All of me, Lord. All I am, all I have, all my works, all my thoughts and all my prayers, the joy in my heart, the pains, heartaches, and unforeseen sufferings I may receive today, my dreams while sleeping and awake, all my love, my mind, my soul, my memory, my will, Lord—my everything.

I come to you, oh Lord, as I am a sinner. I ask you, Lord, please forgive my sinful being. Cleanse me, make me holy and a better servant, to know you more, to trust you more, to love you more, to love your holy Mother Mary more, to love all the angels and saints more, to love my brothers and sisters more, to love my enemies more, and to pray for those who persecute me more.

Take all these, oh Lord, and take all I am and all that is within me. Use them all, oh Lord, in union with your holy Eucharist, with the prayers of the angels and saints and those of my brothers and sisters in you, for the intentions of your divine will, for the salvation of our nation and all nations, for our president and all world and church leaders, for our children and those of the whole world, for each and every soul in purgatory, for our loved ones here on earth and those who have gone before us, for the reparation of all sins, for your healing, Lord, to touch all who have asked me for prayers and for those whom I said I would pray for.

Oh Lord, my God, I ask you, please let your healing continue on each request in my prayer bowl, and I thank you, Lord, for your healing.

I pray, Lord, for your will to be done on earth as it is in heaven, for your will to be done in me this day and all the days of my life until you take me home and continue after my death, and for all of the intentions of our holy Father and our Pope, *Francis.*

Thank you, Lord, for hearing my prayer. I love you, my Lord, my God, my all, my precious Holy Spirit who lives in me, for you are my life. You are my every breath. Amen.

God Forever with Me

My Lord and my God, you are my companion. I do not journey this road alone for you are forever with me. Others cannot see you walking by my side, but I know, for I hear your words so softly speaking within my being, and even when I do not hear your voice within my thoughts, Lord, I know you will never leave me to fight my perils alone. I love you, Lord. Amen.

Surrendering to God

Oh Lord, my God, I do surrender myself to you completely. Lord Jesus, you are the Messiah. Take and change all of me, and make of me as you will. Use me in your divine plan. Your will, Lord, not mine. Your will alone be done in me. Thank you, Lord, for hearing my prayer. I love you, my Lord, my God. Amen.

My Ministry Is Yours

Oh Lord, my God, my ministry is yours. I thank you for using me. You are in charge. I am only a branch. The one who ministers through all I witness in you and through this music inside me is *you*, and I thank you, Lord.

I thank you, my precious Holy Spirit. You who teaches me all things, who writes the music in me, and leads me into all truth.

Lord, I know I am never alone, for you, my Lord, are ever with me, praying, singing, ministering, and touching your people with your healing love.

I thank you, my Lord, for this ministry and for all my blessings, which you, through your mercy and grace, have bestowed on me even though I am a sinner.

Oh Lord, I know I can do nothing unless you, my Lord, will me. I love you, my Lord, and I so deeply desire to forever be singing your praises, ministering to the brokenness and touching your people with your healing love all the days of my life until you take me home and continue after my death forever and always.

I thank you, oh Lord, for hearing my prayer.

I love you, Lord, my God, my all. Amen.

For Guidance

Let it be pleasing to you, oh Lord, what I do this day, that somehow I may bring to all those I meet today, you Lord, in their hearts in some way.

Holy Spirit, guide me. Let your words be on my lips, in my heart, and in my thoughts. Let me not displease you, Lord, and let all I do glorify you, my Lord and my God, this day and all the days of my life until you take me home and continue after my death. Amen.

For Strength

Jesus, my Lord, I pray to be strong in my own journey. I pray through your grace and your mercy, Lord, I may overcome all the devil tempts me with and be all I can be for your glory, oh God, in each and for each of my brothers and sisters in your holy name. Amen.

Come, Holy Spirit

Come, Holy Spirit, deep within my soul. Help me be all I can be for the glory of God. May you, precious Holy Spirit, be the inspiration in all I do throughout my journey! Amen.

Note on My Morning Prayers

These prayers, with which I begin each day of my journey, helps me reach the center of my being, where I can embrace a oneness with God through the grace and mercy of Jesus.

Through God's grace and mercy, I pray these prayers help you seek your own ritual of prayers, these or others, that also helps you reach the center of your own being, where you too can embrace a oneness with God, a deeper relationship with our Father, Jesus and the Holy Spirit, who loves you so much, and desires a oneness with you.

Closing Prayer

I pray we continue to see how God is in each of our daily lives and see His miracles in our lives. I pray we never lose that hunger for God's holy truth. And I pray in making the "sign of the cross," we say it slowly and believe it in our hearts.

In the name of the Father
(who loves me unconditionally)
and of the Son
*(who died for me that I may have
life in its fullness)*
and of the Holy Spirit
(who empowers me in my life).
Amen!

God's love and blessings be yours, my brothers
and sisters, forever and always. Amen.

*May the breath of God breathe on you
and make His presence known!*

Note

Sheila S. Ward
Singer/Songwriter/Author
Evangelist Witness Speaker
Member of the Secular Franciscan Third Order

Songs: www.sheilasward.com
YouTube: www.youtube.com/user/SheilaSWard

About the Author

Sheila is the younger of two children born to devout Catholic parents, Milton F. and Cora D. (Bussiere) Ward (bless their souls). Her Irish twin was Howard M. Ward (bless his soul).

Sheila is a child of God and Mary's child also, and she lives a simple life.

She was singing since age four and a half, and in ministry since 1985, composing over a hundred songs, each coming from a place deep within her being where the eyes of her soul told the story of that part of her journey.

Receiving a call to write this book, *Journey with Trust and Fire Within*, which explains *"why she lives life in the spirit,"* she begins with her deep devotion to Blessed Mother Mary, and why.

She becomes a mother and lives as expected, until the unraveling of her early years brings in the windstorms, then the calm reaches her inner being.

Following God's calling and singing her story throughout her fifteen-year journey in the United States, she eventually was brought back to a Haven in Connecticut, where she met John, her soulmate.

When Sheila reflected on Holy scripture, she couldn't help but notice how these two verses touched her very soul and took root into her own life.

Galatians 2:19-20 *"For through the law I died to the law, that I might live for God. I have been crucified with Christ; yet I live, no longer I, but Christ lives in me; insofar as I now live in the flesh, I live by faith in the Son of God who has loved me and given himself up for me."*

As in all ministries, Sheila begins with the breath of God, a fire within, and saying yes to God's calling. Hallelujah!

CPSIA information can be obtained
at www.ICGtesting.com
Printed in the USA
FFHW021025290919
55242655-60986FF